Two Clouds Too Many

John Moran

Copyright © 2023 by By John Moran

Preface

The following list records some of the major industrial chemical disasters of the last 70 years.

Flixborough, UK June 1974
Seveso, Italy July 1976
Bhopal, India December 1984
Toulouse, France September 2001
Jilin, China November 2005
West, Texas, USA April 2013
Beirut, Lebanon August 2020

There is one place missing from the above list: Killamarsh, an old mining village in North East Derbyshire. Faced with toxic fumes from a waste disposal plant near to their homes, a group of ordinary people formed a protest group. For two years, day and night, they campaigned for their children and grandchildren's right to breathe clean air.

Faced with corporate mismanagement, the inertia of local officialdom and the disinterest of regulatory bodies, the people of Killamarsh never gave up the fight. It was they who made sure that Killamarsh would not be another place added to the list above This is their story.

Contents

CHAPTER ONE	1
A Day Like Any Other	
CHAPTER TWO	18
The First Meeting	
CHAPTER THREE	43
On the March	
CHAPTER FOUR	57
The Grim Reaper and the Toxic Night Shift	
CHAPTER FIVE	71
The Children March	
CHAPTER SIX	88
The Sainsbury's Carrier Bag and the Toxic Ship	
CHAPTER SEVEN	123
The Milkman Gets a Note from Le Président	
CHAPTER EIGHT	133
On the Champs-Élysées	
CHAPTER NINE	151
Minister, Did They Show You the Rocket Fuel?	
CHAPTER TEN	172
Follow the Money	
CHAPTER ELEVEN	185
TNT and the Toxic Package	

CHAPTER TWELVE	190
The Day the Grim Reaper Came to Call	
CHAPTER THIRTEEN	223
Emissions Crackdown	
CHAPTER FOURTEEN	235
Hijack at the Swallow	
CHAPTER FIFTEEN	245
The Dawn Rooftop Protest	
CHAPTER SIXTEEN	259
Houses of Parliament	
CHAPTER SEVENTEEN	275
Strasbourg and Brussels	
CHAPTER EIGHTEEN	287
Yorkshire Television Story of the Year	
CHAPTER NINETEEN	295
One Man and His Dog	
CHAPTER TWENTY	307
Protesters Go to the Polls	
CHAPTER TWENTY-ONE	319
People Power	
CHAPTER TWENTY-TWO	323
The Days of Reckoning	
CHAPTER TWENTY-THREE	329
Life After RASP	

CHAPTER ONE

A Day Like Any Other

This is a story about my community, the village of Killamarsh in North East Derbyshire. Let me introduce myself: my name is John Moran and I was the local milkman. At the time my story starts, I had lived in this village for 20 years; I was married to Sandra and we had three children Jonathan, Julian and Faye. In 1984, after working for Express Dairy in Sheffield, I decided to buy my own milk round, and that's how I came to be Killamarsh's milkman.

In 1998, the village was still recovering from the devastating closure of its two pits, the High Moor and Westthorpe collieries, and the savagery of the Thatcher government of the 1980s. Ex-miners had now been forced into jobs that paid far less and had virtually no trade union representation.

Killamarsh is not a pretty place. If you approach from the south of Sheffield through Halfway, an industrial estate over the narrow bridge crossing the River Rother, you come under the old steel railway viaduct that once carried the coal from this former mining village in another era when times were more prosperous. Once under this bridge you pass the Midland pub on your right, and on the left the Juniors working men's club. Further on you pass rows of terraced houses before reaching the main street, Bridge Street; this leads up to the White City, so called because that was the original colour of the houses before mining and industry changed them to grey. Back on the main road, at the bottom of Bridge Street, you then carry on through our village to the top of Lock Hill, crossing the now disused Chesterfield to Worksop canal. The Killamarsh Junior School is on the left and the Infants school is on the right. My house stood just beyond the schools, on the corner of Belklane Drive. A little further on is the roundabout where one road takes you to Mansfield and the other – to the left – takes you to Rotherham. Half a mile along the Rotherham Road you pass a white building, the Angel Inn; just after this on the left is the entrance to Ellisons Road. After another 50 yards you cross the border between Killamarsh and Rotherham, and then you can turn left and enter the Rother Valley Country Park. The road leads you down to the lakes and the watersports facilities. In 1998, after two hundred yards you would have seen a huge incinerator on the left, formerly belonging to Leigh Environmental but in January 1998 having been taken over by SARP UK. They were a subsidiary of Vivendi, also known as Générale des Eaux, a multinational French company employing 325,000 people worldwide. Leigh Environmental, a chemical waste-processing company, had taken over the site in the early 1980s – it had originally been a tar works. For almost 20 years, Killamarsh had lived in fear of its neighbour on the edge of the Rother Valley. Only those who have lived so near to a huge chemical waste plant will fully understand what daily life was like here; for all who have not, I will try to explain.

Our children at the Sheffield Road schools, across the road from my house, had lady volunteers who had a very particular duty, or as we called them, 'Sniffer Patrols'. When the children were outside in the playground, time and time again they were covered in black or orange clouds, with terrible smells. Children with tears running down their cheeks, but they are not crying; they cough and splutter, but they don't smoke; they get blisters on their faces where there were none minutes before. Residents who have to bring their children back into the house on summer's days because the same clouds are once again shrouding the village, barbecues abandoned, picnics cancelled. Windows firmly closed on summer evenings, drains in the road that released toxic smells that almost keeled you over as you walked past them, due to the chemicals having been discharged into the sewers from this waste plant. Teaching assistants who have to carry trays of inhalers to the children before they go on a nature walk – we estimated in 1998 that 60 percent of our children had asthma.

In 1986 we had had a serious explosion when a huge diesel tank caught fire less than 200 yards from the Sheffield Road Junior School. In the diesel tank were stored PCBs, or to give them their full name, polychlorinated biphenyl – a carcinogenic compound that has since been banned due to its harmful nature.

May 14, 1998 seemed like any other Thursday, but it would change the lives of many in our village forever. For me it was an early morning start at 3.00 am, then back home for 9.00 am and a couple of hours' sleep before going back out to collect my money for the milk round. It was a lovely May day with clear blue skies; at about 4.30 pm I had just collected a customer's money on Kirkcroft Lane. I turned to leave and there on the horizon, towards the Rother Valley Country Park, was a huge orange cloud rising at least 300 feet into the air and drifting over the village from SARP UK. I packed up my collecting for that Thursday early and decided to head home. The whirr of helicopters overhead told me that, whatever it was, it was pretty serious. When I reached the top of the road at the roundabout, I found police cars blocking all the roads back into the village. I asked a burly policeman what was going on, and his reply was short and to the point. "SARP have had a tanker full of acid explode."

"I want to get through," I said.

"Sorry, sir, no one is allowed into the village."

"I live down there – it's only 50 yards," I argued.

"Okay, but make sure you stay in and lock all your windows," were his parting words as I weaved my way through the police barricades. As I pulled up, I saw all my neighbours and their children running outside to listen to what the police in the helicopters were trying to say. They were in fact trying to tell us to stay inside and lock all our windows, but no one could hear because of the engine noise. The curfew lasted until 9.45 that night, and for four hours no one entered or left our village.

The next day the whole village was discussing the incident. Carol Dye, a mum of two who lived on the White City, told me, "We had to run for our lives, John. We were in the Rother Valley when we saw the orange clouds, they seemed to be all over us – how long are we going to keep taking this crap from them? One day this village will just get blown away." Carol was about 28, 5ft tall at the most. She was a person who in different circumstances could have achieved so much more than her present situation. She was married to Terry, a nice, quiet guy, unable to understand the complex character of his steely, independent wife. She was also a great singer, as the many clubs and pubs in the area would testify. She was a child born into tough times: the miners' strike, soup kitchens... childhood memories are not the same for all of us. I didn't know it on that day, but our paths would cross many times over the next two years. She was an amazing, fearless young lady.

"Sorry, I don't know. We were here ten years ago – remember what happened then?" was my reply.

"I will tell you what happened then – sweet FA. Bloody councillors, MPs and the Environment Agency sold us down the river, told us to leave it to them, to all go on home." One thing about Carol, she said it as it was, which did not suit everyone in our village. She could be too direct, but that was Carol Dye.

She was right, though. A decade earlier, after the other explosion when the huge diesel tank containing the PCBs gave off deadly dioxin clouds over the schools, we had all attended a public meeting called by Derbyshire County Council. The meeting was held at the Sheffield Road Junior School. That night in 1986, there was a lot of anger in the room, people were frightened for the safety of their families, especially their children who attended these two schools so close to the plant. Lone voices with the courage to speak up shouted at the councillors and the Environment Agency officers to take action against Leigh Environmental. They were the brave ones; most of us didn't say a word, listening politely like English people do. The lone voices were smothered, the councillors told us that they would sort this problem out and they would in the future oppose the renewal of licences for Leigh, the Environment Agency would monitor the site and step up their inspections. The meeting ended and we all trooped home.

"That is not the way we are going to get the place shut up," were the first words Sandra, my wife, said as we walked back home feeling deflated. I felt regret at not having had the courage to stand up and say what I thought, but that was what I was like. I suppose I didn't like to speak up in a crowd. "We need to take more action, we need to protest, we need to get nasty – that's what we need to do."

I listened to Sandra's words, and I knew as usual she was right. I had met her in 1969 and we were married in 1970 – our relationship had been to say the least pretty stormy over the years, but Sandra's greatest quality, one that is not found in everyone, was a fierce loyalty to me and anyone she called a friend. She was very direct, did not waste words, her perception of people and situations always spot on. Another woman with her own mind, like Carol Dye, one who you would want on your side when you are in a battle.

The week after the explosion of May 14, 1998, there was much talk in the village about what happened after the incident, including reports of SARP's on-site hose being full of holes. The fire crew had to bring their own in because they were unable to use those on site.

"About right for Leigh's" – that was the greeting I got from Brian Ashmore as I delivered on Ashley Lane early on the Tuesday morning. Locals still referred to the place as Leigh's even though it was now SARP UK. "Do you know, John, they didn't even ring the emergency services? It took someone on the Norwood estate to ring them; they didn't get a call till two hours after the explosion. Nothing's changed much down there, has it?"

"No. I don't think so. only more of the same," I replied. Brian had been the school caretaker and had witnessed the scenes of the Sniffer Patrols, mornings when he could not breathe whilst working in the early hours. He was not a well man, small and slight, with a gaunt face under a black beret that he always seemed to wear. Brian was a quiet man, but as I was to find out, a man I would come to admire for his courage over the next two years. Brian was married to Margaret; they were both in their sixties at the time and had two sons, one working for some big electronic company in France, the other, Jonathan, married and lived in the village. Margaret had been a nurse for many years, she was well-spoken, smart and just as angry as Brian. She came out just as I was about to drive away.

"What a state our village is in, John. Do you know how many of our neighbours here on Ashley Lane have died from cancer these last ten years?"

"Yes, I know there is a lot, why do you think that is?" I asked.

"The reason is," Brian chipped in, "the lane is in a direct line from the incinerator chimney; the plume falls directly on to it. They will deny any responsibility – they always have, always will."

I left them both. There were a lot of angry people in our village. Would it all blow over, so to speak, and just simmer below the surface as it had done for so many years? One thing I did know – it would not be our Derbyshire Council or the Environment Agency that we would turn to. We had turned to them once before.

It was about 8.00 pm on the following Friday. I had just finished collecting for the day when I stopped outside the Crown pub on Kirkcroft Lane, opposite the village church, a stone-built building standing on the corner with Ashley Lane.

"Evening, John."

"Evening, Roger," I replied. Roger Barraclough was mine host at the Crown, having been there for a few years. An ex-miner, he was someone who had seen the miners' strike at first hand having been employed at the local pits, Westthorpe and High Moor collieries, now long closed. Roger was a big guy, stood no messing in his pub, but he was a nice bloke. His mother Beryl was a customer of mine for years, and was known by generations of village children as the lollipop lady who helped them safely cross the road. A lady, yes, that's how I would describe her – I can say no more. Roger's brother was a headmaster somewhere near Brough in the Lake District. Over a half a beer the talk soon turned to SARP.

"I see Harry Barnes MP has been meeting managers and workers," said someone to my right.

"Hello, Terry," I said as I turned. Terry Turner was another ex-miner, about the same age as me, mid fifties. Dead straight was Terry, a thorn in the side of our Council. He and his wife Myra had been in a previous protest group in the village.

"If he does as much as he did in 1986, then he shouldn't have bothered."

"The trouble in 1986, Terry, was that we were all too nice – don't upset the Council, the MP and the EA." Roger's statement said it all. We all knew where we had gone wrong. Would anything be different this time, would *we* be different this time? Time would tell.

Saturday was my favourite day. I always liked sport – football, but especially horse racing. I was an apprentice jockey in the 1950s and 60s at Epsom and Malton and never got it out of my system. I would get done on my round for about 9.30 am, then back home to study my racing paper. There would not be much time to study this Saturday, May 30. I was in the house about 11.00 that morning when I heard people shouting outside. I went out to see what all the commotion was about. It was happening all over again. There in the sky was another 300-foot plume of orange clouds coming from SARP UK. Once more the helicopters whirred overhead, the same police barricaded our village, once more we were under curfew. The front-page headlines in the *Sheffield Star* that night said it all – "Never Again". The paper went on to describe how 20,000 people had to take cover. The huge shopping centre at nearby Crystal Peaks had to be sealed off, keeping hundreds of shoppers inside for fear of the mixture of nitric acid and hydrofluoric orange clouds that were covering the buildings.

The next day, Sunday, all talk was of the latest incident; it seemed that was all any of us talked about these days. SARP not only took all the air you breathed, it was now taking over all our conversation as well. After breakfast, at about 11.00 am, I saw two or three people putting out leaflets. I went to retrieve the one in my postbox. The words leapt off the page: "How long are the people of Killamarsh going to accept this situation?" It went on, "After two huge explosions and incident after incident is it not time to do something?" It was then I saw him for the first time. In his early thirties, tall at over six foot with steely blue eyes, and gaunt, as if food was not a priority – this was Alistair Tice. He was a member of the Socialist Party and told me his party was interested in helping the village.

"Might be a problem with the Socialist Party," I said, "lots of people think they are a bunch of anarchists."

"Well, all the other people haven't helped you in the past – have you got anything to lose?"

"They are having a public meeting down at the Village Centre next Tuesday, we will have to see what they say, I suppose," was my reply.

He turned and walked away. I had a feeling that our paths would cross again.

Tuesday evening came, and with hundreds of others we headed for the Village Centre. When we arrived the place was nearly full and it was still half an hour until the start of the meeting. At 8.00 the place was full to capacity, people having to stand outside to try to get a view of the proceedings inside. At the top table were all the local councillors: Alan Charles, Jayne Holden, Bob Harper, Colin Robinson and Grant Laughton, flanked by Environment Agency and Health and Safety officers from Sheffield. The meeting was opened by Alan Charles, who said that they were deeply concerned by the events of the last weeks and the Derbyshire County Council would be meeting SARP UK management in order to sort things out. The EA officer said they would be revisiting the site and would be checking more in light of the recent incidents.

"What happened to cause these explosions?" asked Ann Nettleship, who worked at the local supermarket and lived on the White City. The daughter of an ex-miner, Ann was very articulate, a good speaker, another who but for circumstances would have gone a lot further than the cash till at the local Kwik Save. Beside her sat June Cullabine, her sister, smaller in build than Ann. Both would turn out to be like Rottweilers in the years ahead.

"In answer to your question, Ann, I will refer you to the Environment Agency," replied Alan.

"On May 14 a SARP road tanker burst open, releasing its 10-tonne consignment of sulphuric acid and nitric acid, which formed the bright orange cloud that rose into the sky. The second explosion on May 30 at 11.00 am was when a 30-tonne capacity waste storage tank suddenly split open, spilling a mixture of hydrofluoric acid, nitric acid and hydrochloric acid and releasing another bright orange cloud."

"Is it true that all SARP's hoses had holes in, and the same hoses were still there when the second explosion happened, that they had not replaced them?" Ann asked, determined that she would make it clear to all present what an irresponsible company SARP was.

"We cannot confirm that at the present time," was the Environment Agency officer's guarded reply.

This brought jeers from the packed audience; they knew it was right. You couldn't keep secrets like that in a close-knit village like ours.

"The lady at the back with her hand up." Alan Charles, the chair, invited a lady in her sixties to speak.

"I am Wendy Wellings." Wendy had had connections with our village for a long time. She had once been the landlady of the Crown, and her daughter Louise lived in the village close to SARP UK on Rotherham Road. The day Louise found her car enveloped by one of the orange toxic clouds would transform the life of this tiny, fearless 29-year-old mother. "I have my daughter and two grandsons live near this plant – what I want to know is how many complaints have been made and logged in your records over the last 12 months and how many times have you found any cause or reason for these complaints."

The EA officer thought for a moment, then said, "Sorry, I don't have that information to hand."

"Well, I have it for you." Producing a document from a folder, Wendy went on, "From May 8, 1996 to May 30, 1998, there were more than 70 complaints received, complaints as diverse as two to three weeks of pungent odour to an awful smell like paint stripper to a smell of burning bodies. This document—" waving the papers in her hand "—is your own record of complaints and action taken, in most the usual answer has been, 'Odour not traced, no unusual activities on site.' Not once in 70 complaints did you resolve any single complaint or give a reason to the caller. It beggars belief that you, the Environment Agency, who are supposed to protect us from such dangers posed by a company like Leigh Environmental, now SARP UK, to our community have failed to do so." To rousing cheers from the packed audience, Wendy sat down.

Once again Alan Charles invited someone to speak, this time a woman in her twenties, Allison Sampson. Married to Kevin with a young daughter Charlotte, really she was not a Carol Dye type. I always thought she was a bit on the soft side.

"I would like to ask what is the response to the fact that I have had three miscarriages in the last four years, that many of my friends have miscarried, that we are having babies born with abnormal medical conditions – blindness, club feet and Down Syndrome, far above the average for a village of our size. We have been told that living near a chemical waste plant increases the chances and lots of us believe that the cause is the SARP UK plant."

"There is no proof that this company is responsible," the Health and Safety officer responded.

"The proof is in our village," was the response from several members of the audience.

The chair, Alan Charles, said that he would ask Jayne Holden of the District Council to speak on the behalf of the Killamarsh and Derbyshire County Council.

"We all know how strongly you all feel, but you must leave this to us. We intend to oppose the renewal of their licences and the Environment Agency is going to increase their inspections of this site. You all can rest assured your elected councillors will sort this out."

"Like you did in 1986?" shouted Ann Cockerill. The local playgroup was run by Ann; she wouldn't win any popularity contests, being very direct with what some had found a sharp tongue, but like a few of the women I have already mentioned, she was passionate about the welfare of the kids in her village, and especially the toddlers in her playgroup.

With that Alan Charles said, "I will bring this meeting to a close, thank you for attending this evening."

The audience was just about to rise when a tall man in the second row stood up and, turning to face the crowd, I recognised him. I had met him once before – it was Alistair Tice. He spoke in a calm and strong voice, "Is this what you all want – 1986 all over again? These people had their chance to get rid of this waste plant with its toxic waste incinerator.

They haven't done it in the last twelve years, do you trust them again?"

"No, no, we don't," many voices answered as one.

"Well, the only way is that you, the people, will have to do it on your own, you will have to organise yourselves."

"How on earth can we close it on our own? This is a multinational company, it employs nigh on 300,000 people – it can't be done." One person had said what we all thought.

"How do we start?" I heard myself blurting out – that was the first time I had ever spoken up. Things were beginning to change.

Alistair continued, "We need to hold a meeting to discuss how we should move forward. Does anyone know where we could hold a meeting?"

"You can hold it at my pub, the Crown on Ashley Lane. I have a room upstairs that holds 100 or so, should be OK." Roger Barraclough had come up aces.

We had begun.

Chapter Two

The First Meeting

The first meeting at the Crown was arranged for Thursday June 4 at 7.30. Word quickly spread through the village and a good turnout was expected. As I made my way to the Crown that night, I wondered, where do you start? I had no idea – I would have to wait and see.

The Crown was packed with people when we arrived. We had come with Terry and Myra Turner and Myra's close friend Brenda Glossop. Brenda had also been in the protest group KRAC (Killamarsh Residents' Action Committee) with Terry and Myra in 1986 after the fire. Quiet and fairly reserved, she lived near Myra in Primrose Close, close by the schools and even closer to SARP UK. She worked as a dinner lady at the school alongside Myra; they both were members of the 'Sniffer Patrol'. Also at the meeting that night were another two members of KRAC, David and Margaret Parr. David was a self-employed businessman with interests in garden centres. They had been unsuccessful in 1986, but like the others who had been in that group, were here once again to resume the battle. Margaret, like several other women in RASP, would prove to be a fearless campaigner.

We all huddled together in the upstairs room. It probably did hold a hundred, but two hundred was pushing it a bit. At the top table sat Alistair Tice. "Good evening to you all," were his opening words. "My name is Alistair Tice. Tonight we are here to organise ourselves in order to close SARP UK." As the cheers and applause died down, he went on to say, "SARP UK will not be easy to close; they are a multinational company with vast resources, money, political influence and PR companies whose job it is to protect this company from any adverse publicity. That is what they have – what have we got? A group of ordinary people in an old mining village. What occupations have we?"

The packed assembly replied variously: "Window cleaner," "Painter," "Dinner lady," "Railway driver," "Care worker," and of course, "Milkman" was my response.

"What wealth have we got?" continued Alistair. There were blank looks all round. "We have no wealth then, and not much political influence."

"Not much hope, either," said one doubting voice in the audience.

"Oh no, not at all," responded Alistair. "What we have is Right and the Truth, and all we need is a group of dedicated people who are committed to the cause. This will be no easy battle: some of you will go where you have never been before, do things that you never thought you would do, say things that you never thought you would say, but if we stick together, we will succeed where many have failed over the last decades in this village. We have to show this company that we will not go away, we will have to confront them at every opportunity, exploit their errors, we have to sustain a campaign with little or no money, only the thought that one day we will have the incinerator taken from the village and in so doing protect the future health of our children and grandchildren.

"What we must first do is to form an action committee, with everyone having a particular title and role to play, so let's get on with that. First we need a Chairman."

Kevin Jones, a self-employed local businessman, was duly elected. Secretary was Faye Moran, Treasurer Pat Whitehouse, Vice Chairman Roger Barraclough, Campaign Officer – Alistair Tice was the only one for that job. After several more positions had been filled, Alistair looked down the at the list.

"Just one more job left – Press Officer." No one responded.

I stood up and said, "I will do that." If I thought that I had picked a soft job, time would tell I was a long way short of the mark.

It was now around 9.30 pm and the meeting was about to finish when Alistair asked, "Are we up for staging our first protest?"

"Yes!" was the unanimous reply from the audience. With that we all made our way to our cars and a convoy drove through the village. That June evening was warm and as we drove down Rotherham Road, turning left into Ellisons Road towards SARP UK, the smell of the site met us as we turned the corner, that obnoxious plastic odour that the residents will forever associate with Leigh and now SARP. We all drove up to the main gates that had been left open as usual in order that the toxin-carrying tankers and waste-carrying vehicles could enter and leave the site 24 hours a day. We closed the road – nothing could go in and nothing could come out. For most of us who had never protested in our lives, it was a strange, uncomfortable feeling, it was for me anyway, but it was different for the women in the group – they felt anger, they saw SARP UK as something that threatened everything a mother holds dear. The security men didn't know what to do. They didn't know whether to lock the gates or call the police; they had never seen hundreds of protesters at the gates before. Then the chanting started, "SARP UK, take your toxic crap away!" a cry that would be heard many times over the next two years, from the dark and smelly Ellisons Road to the tree-lined boulevards leading to SARP's parent company Vivendi in the shadows of the Champs-Élysées in Paris.

During a break from the chanting someone said, "We are a protest group without a name – does anyone have any ideas?"

Several names were suggested, some ridiculous, some obscene, then Pat Whitehouse, our newly appointed treasurer, said, "Why not call ourselves RASP?"

"What does that stand for?" someone asked.

"Residents Against SARP Pollution, an anagram of SARP."

RASP seemed the perfect name, and from then on that was how we would be known.

The time was now 10.30 pm and the night was about to come to an end, when the sound of police sirens and flashing blue lights appeared at the other end of Ellisons Road. Five or six police cars pulled up.

"Just like Sheffield buses, none, then they all come together," was Brian Ashmore's response to the sight of our 'finest'.

"What's this all about?" the self-appointed police spokesman asked, then continued, "Clear the road of all these vehicles, you are causing an obstruction and stopping the company operating."

"Exactly what we want and intend to do," shouted Carol Dye. She was on familiar ground; she didn't mind the confrontation. Carol was like a lot more in our village, a child of the miners, those same miners who had battled the Thatcher government and the police not six miles from where we stood tonight at the now infamous 'Battle of Orgreave' on June 18, 1984. The miners' only crime was fighting for their jobs and, like RASP were now, for their community. Carol knew, as we all did, that confrontation was the name of the game.

More police arrived. We decided to call it a draw and all trooped to our cars – we had made our first protest, we had stopped vehicles entering and leaving the site. The battle had now begun. Just before we departed, Alistair came to me and asked if we could meet the following morning. I said I usually had a couple of hours' sleep after my round then I could meet with him.

The next morning, I had just had breakfast when a knock on the door announced the arrival of Alistair. "Hope I am not too early?" he said.

"I don't think so – I have already done my day's work," was my reply.

"Down to business, then. You might not know it, John, but your job of press officer is crucial. Whether we are to succeed or fail to close this company will ride on how good we are with the media; we need to expose every error this company makes or has made in relation to the people of

Killamarsh. Every interview you do with the media – the TV, radio and the press – will be scrutinised by this company. Every error we make will be seized upon by SARP UK and they will crucify us. They are paying a PR company thousands to make sure that they do just that. You are the person that will front this protest, there will be a lot riding on you. The only thing I would say is that SARP UK are trying to defend a lie, you will be speaking the truth, never forget that."

Alistair's words would stay with me over the next two years; they were words I would always call upon when things were not going well, when things were looking bleak, when I grew weary from days and nights without sleep in our determination to close this company and its toxic waste incinerator down.

"I want you to meet someone tomorrow, John – Ken Coates, Euro MEP." He had been Labour MP for Mansfield for 28 years, a good man, Tony Blair got rid of him as he was too far to the left for Blair's New Labour. Coates' office said they would help with the printing of leaflets and posters, and Ken would bring it to the attention of Brussels. He would be in the village the next day to try to arrange a meet.

"What are we going to do today?" I asked.

"Well, I think that we should picket SARP UK down at their gates. They are have are having a meeting of management with police, fire and health services. We should make our presence felt; also, we should try and get the media there. If you can see to that, it will keep the story going – that is what you will have to do from now on."

With that Alistair left. "See you down there then, about 3.30, I will contact the telephone tree!" he called as the gate swung behind him.

The telephone tree was introduced at the recent RASP meeting. We would ring six people, who in turn rang six more – this way we could ensure a quick response to any situation, invaluable in the protests that were to come. That afternoon I passed the Angel pub and turned the corner into Ellisons Road, passed the huge scrapyard of Brian Hull on the right, and down the road to the gates of SARP UK. The road was full of RASP protesters, banners waving. The slogan 'SARP UK OUT' was everywhere. Steve Martin's flat-back lorry was across the gates. Steve was a self-employed haulage driver, married with two small children, he lived on Rotherham Road very close to the plant. His two sisters Julie and Samantha, who were on our RASP committee as publicity officers, would become leading protesters in the coming year or so. "That will stop them from coming in or out for a bit, John," were his words. That was already something of a understatement. We had about eight huge tankers backed up all the way down Ellisons Road waiting to get back on site, also about four trying to leave the plant. The protesters had to put up with the fumes from all the tankers, which were green with a broad white strip round the front with the words 'SARP UK' in yellow on the sides. Add that to the plastic chemical smell that was coming from the site and it was not a pleasant place to be.

"Have they started the meeting?" I asked Steve.

"Don't know, John, nothing seems to be happening at the moment."

Suddenly I noticed a Yorkshire Television van and crew approaching. I had already informed them of our protest, as well as the *Sheffield Star* newspaper, the local rag *Eckington Leader* and the *Derbyshire Times*, determined that every time we did anything in this campaign we would carry the media with us every step of the way. There would be nobody for many miles and further that had not heard of the fight that RASP were in with SARP UK.

"Are you John Moran?" one guy said as he held out his hand.

"Yes," I hesitantly replied. "Press Officer for RASP, that's me."

"Have you got anything to say as to why you are here today?" At the same time the TV cameraman turned his lens on me.

"We are here today to let this company know that we want them to cease all operations and close this plant down."

"What is going on today?" asked the reporter.

"There is a meeting: the management of SARP UK are meeting fire, police and health services," I replied.

"Is there any common ground that you would be prepared to meet with this company?" he asked.

"There will be no compromise with SARP UK. The days of compromise are long gone for our village; we don't trust them and we want them out."

With that, the 100 or so protesters waved their banners, chanting, "SARP UK, hear us say, take your toxic crap away!"

As the chanting died down, the reporter, Steve Caddy, said, "People are saying you have no chance of closing this plant and having this incinerator took down, you are wasting your time. This is a multinational company and there is no way you can win. What would you say to those people?"

"My answer is that it is us or them. We will not stop our protests, not stop disrupting this site, we may well be here for a long time. RASP is determined and in the end we will succeed."

The guy with the camera closed in with his lens and the reporter concluded, "There are a lot of angry, determined protesters outside the premises of SARP UK today; I have a feeling that this story is just beginning. I return you to the studio of Yorkshire Television."

An hour later the word was passed to us that SARP UK had, because of the protesters, earlier transferred the meeting to Mosborough Hall. They had underestimated the strength of RASP – we had people from the village who supported us in every shop, every workplace, every office and every business in the area. Hence the phone call from Mosborough Hall tipping us off about the change in venue.

On hearing the news all the protesters headed for Mosborough Hall. This place was a pretty high-class hotel about three miles from Killamarsh, on the left of the Sheffield to Barlborough road. We drove up the tree-lined drive to the entrance, me in my Volkswagen transporter milk van. We must have looked quite something. Early light rain had now turned into a downpour. We piled into the entrance where they immediately locked the doors. The chanting started up again: "SARP UK, hear us say…"

I went up to the front door and rung the bell, Ann Cockerill standing beside me. "I want to speak at the meeting that they are having with SARP UK," I told the young man they had sent out to try to calm us down.

"Sorry, sir, this is a private function and only invited guests are allowed."

We were definitely not on SARP UK's invite list, I couldn't argue with that.

"We are not bothered about invited guests." Ann was in no mood to turn round. "We are coming in and you and everyone are not going to stop us."

With that we all piled into the reception. We were soon joined by the hotel manager, who said that if we made one more step he would call the police.

"Call them, they are only in the next room." Alistair's voice, clear as a bell, came across the reception area.

"You will have to arrest us all!" shouted Carol Dye.

More protesters pushed into the reception area, all like drowned rats with steam and the smell of rain-drenched clothes everywhere. This was not what the manager of the Mosborough Hall hotel wanted, and the sight of the Yorkshire TV crew trying to get in on the act only gave him visions of his worst nightmare. At that moment we were joined by another member of the hotel staff, who whispered to the manager something we were unable to hear.

"I have to inform you that the meeting has been abandoned, that all the people in attendance have left by the back entrance."

"Cowards, cowards!" was the cry.

"Just like SARP – never face us, never speak to us." Tony Ward's words said it all. Tony, a retired railway driver in his late sixties, with children and grandchildren in our village, had more reason than most to be here today, and he would become a prominent RASP protester in the coming two years.

That night, I watched with interest as the introduction to Calendar News came on Yorkshire Television. After saying,

"Today at the controversial chemical waste plant at Killamarsh where there have been two serious explosions," they showed the pictures of the two huge orange clouds that had covered our village. They went on to say, "We have had our reporter there, we now go to the site in Killamarsh." There we were outside the gates, banners waving, crowds chanting, the tankers all backed up in the site and all the way up Ellisons Road. They then did the interview with me. Everyone gets fifteen minutes of fame, or so they say – maybe I had just got mine.

The next day Alistair rang. "Great start, John, saw the television last night, front page of the *Sheffield Star* all about the protest, how we were angry and determined to close SARP, but later editions are carrying the story about the abandoned meeting at Mosborough Hall."

"Well, that's great – two for the price of one," I replied.

"I will see you later, John." With that he put the phone down.

Later that day, I had just returned from an extra delivery, having missed a couple of customers with their morning milk. I hoped that lack of sleep did not make me start to neglect my business. As I stepped down from the van I heard, "Good morning, John." Alistair's voice jolted me from thoughts of sleep and milk rounds.

"Morning, Alistair."

"I want you to meet Ken Coates."

At Alistair's side was a small, stocky man with large-rimmed glasses. "Pleased to meet you, John. I wanted to convey my message to all at RASP to say how we all at my office in Mansfield admire what you are all trying to do here in Killamarsh."

"Thanks, Mr. Coates, I will let all our members know at our next weekly meeting."

"I also want you all to know that my office will be able to help with your leaflets and printing," he continued.

"I know we only have about £27 in the funds, we collected it at the protest at SARP, so that would not get us very far," I replied.

With that Ken Coates and Alistair left. I had just met a man whose life had been built on social justice for everyone, a dying breed, Ken, his like sadly disappearing with the years from the political scene.

The telephone rang later that day. "It's Alastair." By now there was no need to say this, I knew his voice. "We must call a meeting at the Crown for tomorrow night, Friday, we have to do something this weekend to keep up the pressure. Don't want to ease off now the story's running. Can you ask Roger if we can use the room? I will get the telephone tree on the go."

"OK. I will only phone you if there is a problem with the room – don't think there will be. I will book it for 7.30." With that we both hung up.

The Crown was packed that night, as we all huddled again in the upstairs room. Kevin Jones, our chairman, opened the meeting. "I must say, what a great week we have had: the protest at SARP after the meeting here last week, followed by the protest in the week, followed by Mosborough Hall. Television, *Sheffield Star*, *Eckington Leader* and now front page of the *Derbyshire Times* – I think that we can give ourselves a round of applause." The cheers and clapping that followed reflected the mood of the group.

Then Alistair stood up. "Ideas, that is what we want. Anybody got any ideas what we can do this weekend?"

"Well, there's the Water Ski Championships at the Rother Valley Country Park on Sunday and Monday, it being the bank holiday, there should be lots of visitors," came the voice of Brenda Hancock.

"That seems a great idea, we need to leaflet all the cars as they come into the Rother Valley," replied Alistair. "We would be best if we stood near the office where they have to pay – they are already slowing down and stopping, it should be no problem and its right opposite SARP UK." He then added, "What about having a petition for them to sign, asking for this company to cease all operations and vacate the site? The more signatures we get in the coming months the stronger our case will be."

"When can we have the leaflets ready for, Alistair?" asked Kevin Jones.

"Well, if we work through the night we should have them done for Sunday morning early. I will get in touch with Becky." Rebecca Fryer, or Becky as she was known, was a close friend of Alistair, a leading Socialist Party member and would be a key campaigner for RASP in the years to come.

"Anything else before we close? Any more ideas?" asked Kevin.

It was Steve Martin that answered. "Yes, I have one – what we need is a symbol of RASP, something that everyone will associate with RASP, something not stupid, but serious."

"Have you anything in mind, Steve?" asked Alistair.

"Well, I was walking past the fancy dress shop in the village and in the window was a costume of a Grim Reaper with a scythe in his hand; I thought it would be great to have someone wear it and lead us when we are protesting and marching."

"Does anyone know the owner?" asked Kevin.

"I do, I will see what I can do, I know that she supports the campaign," I replied.

When I had finished my round on the Saturday I pulled up outside the fancy dress shop on Sheffield Road. The owner had been a milk customer for a few years and I knew her quite well. I closed the door behind me and entered a world of make-believe, all sorts of costumes for every occasion. It was an unusual shop to be found in a small village.

I spotted him right away in the corner. There stood the Grim Reaper costume and mask with his scythe in his hand.

"I have come for him," I told her, pointing at the Grim Reaper, "I want him to lead our marches and protests, a symbol that if we ignore SARP UK, he will be waiting, but it depends how much it will cost to rent."

"Before we sort that out, John, I want to tell you what happened to my two dogs after the SARP leaks. They were always fed outside, and the day of the leaks we left them in the back garden. Within three days they were both in the vets, one died and the other only just survived. I have been told of ducks being found dead on the Rother Valley, a woman on the Norwood estate had her two pet rabbits die within days of the orange nitric acid clouds and all the hedges on the estate had the appearance of being burnt. The sooner we get them shut down and the incinerator moved the better."

I told her how sorry I was to hear about her two dogs and hoped that the survivor would make a full recovery.

"Oh, the Grim Reaper, the rate is…" I held my breath – we only had £27 in the RASP funds. "…The rate is nothing to RASP, keep him and bring him back when it's all over and you have closed down SARP UK."

"It may be quite a while," I replied.

"You have him for as long as it takes."

I thanked her on behalf of RASP and hurried back to the milk van. We had just recruited another RASP member, one that would become a symbol of RASP and a marcher that would seem to take on a near human identity in our fight with SARP UK.

Early Sunday morning Becky Fryer knocked on my door. She had the 2,000 leaflets for the Rother Valley protest and a dozen petition forms with clipboards.

Later that morning found me down on the road to the Rother Valley, opposite the SARP UK incinerator where the RASP protesters gathered as agreed, near the ticket office where the visitors paid. The leaflets told of the two nitric acid leaks and the years of problems with this chemical waste plant and that we were wanting it to be shut down, for the safety not only of our village but for visitors to the Rother Valley Country Park like themselves.

That afternoon we collected the best part of 1,200 signatures on our petition boards and we gave leaflets to every visitor. No one who was asked refused to sign. We had public opinion with us – there is nothing a British person likes more than the underdog and at that moment in time that's what we certainly were.

In the *Sheffield Star* on the next day, Monday, the headlines read: "PROTESTERS DEMAND TOXIC CLOUD ANSWERS." The article went on to say, "Worried Killamarsh residents staged demonstrations outside the Rother Valley Country Park to raise awareness of safety scares at the nearby SARP UK chemical plant." Then it featured interviews with RASP protesters. "A spokesman for SARP UK refuted claims that the area could be unsafe. The emergency services, the fire brigade, the police and also the Environment Agency who are the experts in this field have decided the area around the plant is safe for normal public life.

"The response from from John Moran, spokesman for RASP, was 'We don't trust this company and we don't trust the Environment Agency, with whom SARP have a very cosy relationship. We will be watching this company night and day, we will highlight any errors they make, we will force the EA to police this site, something we know they have not done in years gone by.'"

Monday night was now the regular night for our RASP meetings and just before 7.30 I found myself with Sandra and my daughter Faye walking up to the Crown.

Faye was 25, single, and just returned from living in Los Angeles for the last five years. She was at Sheffield Hallam University studying business management, and had been appointed Secretary for RASP at the formation of the

Action Committee. Faye had good reason to protest – she had been a member of the Hallamshire Harriers athletics team, made famous by the exploits of the Olympian Seb Coe. Faye used to train in the early mornings in the Rother Valley, some mornings choking with the fumes from the then Leigh Environmental. At 25 she had already had a cancer scare.

The Crown was packed as we squeezed into the upstairs room, and Kevin Jones opened the meeting. "Just to say very well done to all of our group who spent the weekend on the Rother Valley, collecting names on the petition – we have over 1,200 – and leafleting the visitors. The story made the front pages once again of the three local papers; we seem to be in the news, either papers or BBC Radio Sheffield or TV every day. What are we organising this week?" Kevin turned to Alistair.

"I have been organising a protest march, here is the poster we have." By "we" he meant with Becky, who had designed it, and the Ken Coates office at Mansfield had organised the printing. The leaflet was A4 size with the headlines:

MASS PROTEST MARCH CLOSE DOWN SARP UK NOW

TAKE KILLER OUT OF KILLAMARSH

On Saturday June 13 we were to assemble in the Kwik Save car park at 10.30 am. The march would begin 11.00 am, and the full route would be going from Killamarsh to halfway then by the Crystal Peaks Retail Park, continuing on through the villages of Sothall and Beighton then entering the Rother Valley Country Park. It would go through the park, passing the watersports centre, and then along the entrance road, turning right onto Rotherham Road then right into Ellisons Road down to the gates of SARP UK on the Norwood Industrial Estate.

The poster stated that we wanted everybody to turn out on this march, including those from neighbouring townships, explaining, "It is our future and our responsibility, together we will succeed." Protesters were encouraged to bring their own banners and placards, and those who could not march were able to meet us at the entrance to the Norwood Industrial Estate at 1.00 pm.

"We have been putting these around the village and all the places the march is going through: it is essential that we get all the villages involved. The more people we get, the more pressure we can put on SARP UK," said Alistair.

"Well done, Alistair and Rebecca, I think you have been brilliant," was Roger's response.

"Does that mean free drinks all round?" asked June Cullabine.

"Steady on, I wouldn't go that far," said Roger with a wry smile. "I will see you all at the Kwik Save car park on Saturday morning 10.30."

"Is there anything else?" asked Kevin as he wound up the meeting.

"Yes," I said. "I have one more item. We will be joined on Saturday by a new member of RASP – they will call him Grim. Grim Reaper."

"Who is going to be Grim Reaper?" asked Tony Ward.

"That will be a secret," I replied, and for the rest of the campaign his identity was never sought by the campaigners. There was a good reason. Grim Reaper in the future would be involved in things that could have seen him arrested and possibly imprisoned.

It was Tuesday following the Rother Valley Protest. I had reason to call at the Post Office in Bridge Street. In the window was a poster – it seemed that the village had a poet. I had heard talk in the past of a poet they called 'Owd Tup', tup being an old Derbyshire name for a sheep. I read on.

A KILLAMARSH PRAYER

As I kneel me down to pray, thank you, Lord, for SARP UK
Whose purpose, so I understand, to keep this green and pleasant land
Safe from all the toxic waste that industry churns out in haste
Recycling all that they are able, all that is non biodegradable

Striving so hard for me and you, making fat profits as they do.

They may well keep this country nice, but why choose us to pay the price?

So Lord, though I don't want to fuss, why let them be so close to us?

Why should we, who live so near, have to live our lives in fear?

Fearing the next toxic cloud, could well be our orange shroud.

Why did you, Lord, let planning fools build their plant so near our schools?

We should feel safe to learn and play, without this constant fear each day

Not have to learn before our teens, what "Suffer little children" means

They say you move in mysterious ways, mysteriously move them far away

And let their presence then be felt, in some stockbroker belt

And see how all the fat cats fare, once SARP's pollutants foul their air.

If on their doorsteps SARP were cast, how long would then the licence last?

Faith moves mountains, so they say. How much to move SARP UK?

Thank you Lord, we're in your care. Thank you for listening to my prayer
We all may, come the next disaster, join you in Heaven so much faster.

The words of 'Owd Tup' a.k.a. Dave Froggatt of Primrose Lane. He lived closer to the plant than anyone else in the village and had good reason to be concerned. His poems would become a part of the RASP campaign in its fight to close SARP UK.

The words of Dave Froggatt, a.k.a. "Owd Tup", were a constant thread during the battle with SARP UK. His poems always struck a chord and got to the heart of the different emotions we had felt over the years about living next door to the toxic plant.

Chapter Three

On the March

Saturday morning I was up at 3.00 am as usual to go down to my refrigerated cold store down on the Norwood Industrial Estate quite close to the SARP UK plant, with my two helpers Chris Dutton and James Edge. We would soon have the round delivered. Both lads, as did three others who helped me on the round, carried inhalers. Five out of five asthma sufferers, 14 and 15-year-olds – what a legacy SARP UK was leaving to our young people. I arrived home, finished for the day, about 9.15 am. It was 10.20 as I made my way down to the Kwik Save car park. The planning that had gone into this march had been huge – Alistair, our campaign officer, our secretary Faye Moran and Becky Fryer all contributed greatly.

Faye had to inform the police, firstly of the route of the march and the distance, giving the organisers' names and the date and start time. All this ensured that the seven-mile march of an expected one thousand people had the help of a heavy police escort. This proved to be essential with the amount of traffic that our march was to encounter.

The sight that greeted me when I arrived was amazing: the car park was filled with protesters, banners waving, placards in hand. The banners said things like, 'Close Down SARP UK' and 'The Future's Not Bright, the Future's Orange', in reference to a well-known phone advert of the time and the orange nitric clouds.

I had already informed all the media, and BBC and ITV camera cars were there as well as Radio Sheffield and the local radio station for Chesterfield, plus all the newspaper reporters. This time *The Yorkshire Post* had sent its reporter to cover the story; this newspaper had the largest circulation of all our local newspapers, covering all of Yorkshire. We were certainly spreading the word.

At 11.00 am the march moved off slowly down Sheffield Road past the bottom of Bridge Street. It was led by two police motorbike outriders and fifty yards in front of them were two police cars, making sure all traffic either gave way or moved to the side. Leading the march proper was the Grim Reaper, scythe in hand. The march took the best part of ten minutes just to leave the Kwik Save car park as it trundled along Sheffield Road. I was the last vehicle in the march, milk van with its sliding doors open to pick up any people who were having difficulty – seven miles was a long way. All along the route at the front of the march I could hear the voice of Carol Dye over the loudhailer.

"SARP UK, HEAR US SAY, TAKE YOUR TOXIC CRAP AWAY!"

RASP had printed and handed out the words to the protest song 'Goodbye SARP UK' and to the tune of 'Dolly Gray' and led by Carol, who was now in full flow, it went like this:

GOODBYE SARP UK

There's something in the air, SARP UK
Can't you sense it everywhere, SARP UK?
There's something in the air, can't you sense it everywhere?
And it's saying "Have a care," SARP UK.

Can you see that toxic cloud, SARP UK?
Shaped just like an orange shroud, SARP UK
Can you see that toxic cloud, shaped just like an orange shroud?
And it shouldn't be allowed, SARP UK.

Why are things so still this morning, SARP UK?
Why did you not heed our warning, SARP UK?
Why are things so still this morning, why did you not heed our warning?
Is it time to start the mourning, SARP UK?

There is something you should know, SARP UK
We're all wanting you to go, SARP UK
There is something you should know, we're all wanting you to go,
For we fear your toxics so, SARP UK.

Why not terminate your lease, SARP UK?
And your operations cease, SARP UK
Why not terminate your lease and your operations cease
So that we can sleep in peace, SARP UK?

Then all the marchers joined in the chorus:

Goodbye, SARP, at last you're leaving
Because we all kicked up a fuss
Goodbye SARP, you'll hear no grieving
It was you or us
When you've gone we'll settle down now

Children can safely play
No need for us to fear and frown, now
Goodbye, SARP UK.

Once again thanks went to our village poet, Owd Tup.

The weather had now turned very wet. Despite this, we marched on, car drivers honking their horns to show their support and people standing clapping at the sides of the roads. We approached the Crystal Peaks shopping centre where all the shoppers were held up in the traffic jams that a march of a thousand people slowly moving along was bound to cause. If there was anybody in the Sheffield and Chesterfield area who did not know RASP by this point, they must have been out of the country for the last five weeks. After passing Crystal Peaks we arrived at Beighton, where many more joined the marchers, and then we entered the Rother Valley Country Park. It was at this point I noticed a stocky man with glasses struggling near the rear of the march.

"Do you want a lift, Mr. Coates?" I shouted.

"Thanks, John, I have never ridden in a milk van before, always wanted to," was his response.

Ken had been the MP for Chesterfield for 36 years before becoming MEP for North East Derbyshire, a true socialist and the last of a wonderful breed now long gone, a man who devoted himself to the working-class people of Chesterfield. He stayed with me for the last half-mile of the march.

"How do you think we are doing with the protest?" I asked.

"You are doing very well involving all the local villages with this march, it will ensure that is just not Killamarsh that is in opposition but all of the south of Sheffield. We are now talking about the best part of 100,000 people."

The march wove its way around the lakes where the recent Water Ski Championships had taken place and, passing the incinerator stack of SARP UK, we then turned onto Rotherham Road, where 50 yards along on the right we entered Ellisons Road onto the Norwood Industrial Estate. It was at this point that we met the shorter march from the Village Centre, which included some Parish Councillors. We all joined together and marched on to SARP UK, Alistair and Carol Dye taking turns on the loudhailer. The roads around the plant were full of banners, placards and protesters.

Alan Charles, Derbyshire County Councillor, led the speeches at the gates of SARP UK. He was the only person on the Council that we at RASP trusted; the other councillors and our MP Harry Barnes we thought had not got the determination to get rid of SARP UK. Alan climbed on to Steve Martin's flat-back truck and, taking the loudhailer from Carol, said, "I think there can be no doubt about the strength of feeling against SARP UK. The number of you who have come to this march is proof of that. I want to say that I have no confidence in this company; their safety record is disgraceful, with incident after incident. I feel that I, like you, would like them to shut down and remove this incinerator from our village. We would like to show by means of a simple experiment how people are affected by these serious leaks that are coming from SARP UK. We have filled one hundred balloons with helium, orange in colour like the recent orange toxic clouds. We are going to release them here today – there is a message to the finder to let us know where they found it." With that the orange balloons were released and everyone watched as they floated away.

Ann Nettleship was the next to speak. "We at RASP are determined that this waste plant will be closed down and removed from the village. We all know how dangerous it is, we all know our community is suffering, the young children with their inhalers, the pregnant mums and the cancer clusters in the village. The Education Authority, the Derbyshire Health Authority, teachers and our local GPs are remaining very quiet; no one is coming forward, RASP is the only voice that is protesting."

To loud applause Ann passed the loudhailer to Alistair.

"You should all have a letter from SARP this week. They have sent out 5,000 letters in which, according to Mark

Stanley, director-cum-PR man, 'We have launched a telephone line to give the people of Killamarsh a clear point of contact, they can use it to get more information or to pass on comments about our operations. We are hosting open days in the near future. We are hoping to reopen all the other operations in phases, once a safety review has been completed for each.'" Alistair continued, "Our response at RASP to Mark Stanley and SARP UK is that you should know we oppose any reopening of any of the processes that are currently suspended, that we will be mounting a 24-hour picket on these gates. Your whole operation will be under the closest scrutiny, long gone are the days you could break the law over leaks and emission levels, we will show what an incompetent company you are running this clapped-out site." To this all the RASP supporters cheered and applauded.

The march started to break up and the protesters began to make their way home.

"I wonder where those balloons will finish up?" I asked, turning to Sandra.

"I don't know, but I know where I will finish up – bed in about ten minutes," she replied. Sandra had just come off a long night shift at Derwent House in Newbold, Chesterfield, where she worked as a care worker for Derbyshire County Council. Like many more in this campaign, it was starting to tire her out trying to work full-time and then spending every spare moment campaigning against SARP. The pressure was on all of us.

That night on the front page of *The Sheffield Star* was the headline 'PEOPLE POWER' and a half-page photo of the march. The story started, "In an amazing show of public opinion, the people of Killamarsh and surrounding areas took to the streets today…"

Today was June 16 – was it really only a month now since the first orange nitric acid cloud had shrouded our village, shutting us off from the outside world? There had been so much happen since then: people I had met, some people I knew well, some I had only known in passing, some people who were until this last month complete strangers to me. I had felt something change in me, no longer afraid to speak up, I was now speaking in front of crowds, doing television and radio interviews. There was for me a feeling of looking in on someone else. Maybe when you have a just cause it does change human behaviour.

"Are you going down tonight?" asked Trevor Cockerill. I had just delivered to the Village Centre; it was about 9.00 am. Trevor was Ann Cockerill's husband, worked as a sales rep for a printing company. Trevor always dropped Ann off for her toddler playgroup held in the Village Centre. Trevor was the complete opposite of Ann, I would describe him as calm and diplomatic, always immaculate whenever you met him.

"Definitely, are you going?" I replied.

"I will see you down here then, starts at 8.00 pm. Reckon I will come for about 7.30, don't want locking out again." This was referring to the previous public meeting when he could not get a seat, and with that he drove away.

As we walked down Lock Hill that evening there were lots of people seemingly appearing from everywhere – all with one destination, the Village Centre. When we arrived, the few remaining seats were being taken; we found a couple near the back of the room.

"Good job we didn't leave it any later, we wouldn't have got in," said Sandra, her face scanning the room as the last few remaining seats were taken up. Yes, the strength of feeling was not dying down, thanks to RASP's efforts – it was increasing. There were almost 500 people, maybe a lot more if you counted the people outside listening to the meeting being relayed by loudspeakers. On the platform was Parish Councillor Jayne Holden, who was nicknamed Lady Jayne by RASP due to her lofty attitude towards us. She had been on the Parish Council for a few years, a staunch Labour supporter, she with her husband John were the mainstay of the Council. They were joined tonight by other Parish Councillors Bob Harper, Colin Robinson and Alan Charles, plus an Environment Officer and Alan Johnson from the government's Health and Safety Executive in Sheffield. Jayne Holden opened the meeting.

"On Monday night at short notice SARP called a meeting with Parish Council members, councillors and others. They dropped the bombshell that they were reopening the secondary liquid fuel plant on Thursday following a safety audit. They said they would not be at tonight's meeting and we were angry, we simply could not believe it. We need to speak to them and them to us but they said after taking advice they would not be attending. I think they should be here tonight apologising for themselves." With that she sat down.

Alan Charles then introduced Alan Johnson, the Health and Safety representative. "Inquiries into the tanker spillage are almost complete and a decision over what action should be taken will follow soon. The investigation into acid spillage is continuing; at the time of the leaks this company operated seven processes at the site, all have been suspended due to the high level of public concern." Mr. Johnson added, "There is little risk from the acid plant outside the company boundary. People have been advised to stay indoors during recent leaks as a sensible precautionary measure."

With that Ann Nettleship of RASP jumped to her feet. Ignoring the protest of the chair, she launched into Alan Johnson. "What a load of rubbish! 'Sensible precautionary measure' – we don't want your whitewash here, a £250,000 fire and police operation is not the response to a 'sensible precautionary measure.' We don't want your bullshit, we want this place shut up."

After this, all of RASP were on their feet. "SARP UK, HEAR US SAY…"

"Order, order!" Alan Charles tried to bring some semblance of restraint to the meeting. "Any more questions?" he asked, trying to move on.

"Yes, I have." A young man in his thirties stood up to speak. "My name is David Milson. I live at Beighton, a village about three miles from Killamarsh down the Rother Valley. We suffer like Killamarsh being so close to this waste plant. What I want to know is can you tell me if the plant that is to reopen on Thursday is the one which gives me a sore throat, is it the one that makes me feel sick, or is it the one that prevents me going outside?"

The blank expression on the face of Alan Johnson was the only response to the questions asked.

"Are there any more questions?" asked Alan Charles. "The lady on the left," he pointed to Margaret Marsh.

Margaret was in her forties, and lived on North Crescent, very close to SARP. She had had a few personal tragedies in her life, the worst when her son who attended the Sheffield Road School was hit by a car on the busy Sheffield

Road and lost his life. Margaret had already spoken to me, being a milk customer. "It's awful here on North Crescent, John," she had told me. "We are so close to SARP, we get the smells and leaks before anyone else. The garden hedges are all burnt away, all the plants in the garden die, all the leaves have brown marks on them, the white shirts you hang out on the washing lines come back with chemical marks all over them." Margaret was one of us.

"What I want to ask is why do Yorkshire Water allow SARP to discharge to the main sewers? You can't go near the grids in our village, you could pass out if you took a deep breath."

The answer from the experts on the platform was more blank looks.

It was at this point that Ken Coates stood up and asked to be allowed to speak. Alan Charles introduced him to the meeting, and Ken explained, "I want to let everyone here know that, at the request of RASP, I have arranged a meeting with the company's managing director in France today to press on him the extent of the local concerns. I am also exploring with Residents Against SARP Pollution what we can do to protect the local people, such as an early warning system."

"Thank you, Mr. Coates," said Alan Charles. The expressions on the faces of all the Parish Councillors did not go unnoticed, they were clearly not happy at the presence of Ken Coates and less at his apparent working together with RASP.

As the meeting was coming to a close, I rose to my feet. "John Moran, press officer for Residents Against SARP Pollution. I want to say in response to the reopening of the SFL plant at SARP on Thursday that we strongly oppose this; they have not waited for the result of the safety investigation to be completed, as usual they are showing a total disregard for this community. RASP will be at the gates on Thursday – the company may well restart, we cannot stop that, what we will do is stop any tanker being able to enter the site or leave it." This was followed by loud cheers from all of the audience, this was no time for weakness and they knew it.

As the noise died down, Jayne Holden rose to her feet. "Confrontation of this sort will get us nowhere – we must settle this problem through the proper channels, we as your elected representatives…" Jayne never managed to finish the sentence, all of RASP and most of the audience were already leaving. If the Council were unaware of the situation before, they were aware of it now. RASP was taking on this company and the the Parish Council had not been invited to the party.

Chapter Four

The Grim Reaper and the Toxic Night Shift

Wednesdays was always an easy day on the milk, having left a double delivery on the Tuesday. The extra hours in bed were a welcome relief – sleep was beginning to get more squeezed as the campaign intensified. Alistair arrived about 11.00 am.

"Morning, John. I've come about Thursday; SARP are going to restart the secondary liquid fuel plant. We have to organise a protest – it will have to be early morning, we want to be able to surprise them because we already have told all the media we are going to be there. They are going to be there waiting for us."

"Well, I think that we should all meet near my cold store on the Norwood Industrial Estate. There is a road leading to SARP's front gates without using the main approach on Ellisons Road," I replied.

Our conversation was interrupted by a knock on my front door; I opened it to find Steve Martin on the doorstep.

"Come in, Steve, you have come at a good time: we are planning an early morning raid on SARP tomorrow morning over their intention to start the SLF plant." We explained that we would approach from behind my unit on the side road and asked if there anything he wanted to add.

"Yes. I have a really thick chain and padlock – I think that we should take it with us and padlock the gates, get the Grim Reaper to do it, then all the CCTV cameras won't be able to pick up who has done it."

"Great idea, Steve, bring the chain. We will get there for about 6.45," I said as I showed them both out.

The next day I started my milk round even earlier than normal at around 2.00 am, described by Sandra as an unearthly time to start work. I wanted to be done in time for the protest. At 6.30 am I arrived back at my cold store unit – the RASP protesters were already there. It was pretty cold that morning for the time of year, and the breath of the protesters was visible in the air. After Alistair had checked that all the RASP members had arrived, about fifty in total who had risen early to march to SARP, I followed him to squeeze down the side of my unit. Pushing our way through wet leaves, nettles and overgrown hawthorn bushes, we were glad to reach open ground again. Alistair and the Grim Reaper led us along the road. Silently we came, the Grim Reaper weighed down with the great chain and padlock. We turned the corner; it was 6.55. The gates of SARP were twenty yards further along on the left. They were locked – they had been expecting us. As we approached, the chanting started up.

"SARP UK, hear us say…"

The Grim Reaper moved towards the locked gates – we didn't even have to close them. What SARP had not understood was that was what we wanted, and we were going to make sure that they stayed locked. When the mayhem we had made had subsided you could see the Grim Reaper had done his work well. The huge chain was securely around the gates and a big padlock held it firmly in place.

The protesters set up all their banners. Samantha and Julie Martin, who were Steve Martin's two sisters, had designed and made a huge banner eight feet high by five feet wide on two poles with foot-high letters: RESIDENTS AGAINST SARP POLLUTION. It would become famous in all our future protests and even on the streets of Paris. They stood with the banner, with all the RASP supporters to the sides. It was not much longer on that early morning before SARP tankers began to arrive, all starting to back up Ellisons Road. At 7.30 am all the night shift were due to leave to go home and the day shift, including office staff and management, were due to start. Then I noticed them – having all been told to get here before 7.15, BBC Television, Radio Sheffield, and Yorkshire Television, plus all the newspaper reporters were there. We would definitely make the news today. Throughout the campaign it would become evident that the media would need little encouragement or persuasion from me to come to our protests – this was a big story in this area and they never wanted to miss being with us. At 7.30 there was complete chaos, workers trying to get out, some workers who needed to get in abandoning their cars up at the top of Ellisons Road and walking the remaining distance to the front gates, only to be confronted by the handiwork of the Grim Reaper. Most of the management were waiting in the Angel pub car park at the top of the road, afraid to confront the protesters outside the gates. It was then that we first saw the blue flashing lights of police cars in the distance, they too were unable to get down Ellisons Road, which was blocked with the waiting SARP tankers. We knew that this would further delay the reopening of SARP. The TV, radio and reporters were having a field day, and had all come across to get quotes from us.

"Why are you protesting today?" the BBC reporter asked me.

"You are not going anywhere today." The sight of tankers backed up along Ellisons Road became a regular feature of the campaign. Our intention was to disrupt SARP's activities in whatever way we could until we achieved our aims. Among those pictured are Margaret Parr and Samantha Williams: there is only one word to describe these ladies – fearless.

"We are here today to oppose the plans SARP have to restart the SLF plant, having said they would not restart any operation until a safety assessment had been done. This has not been done and they are being allowed by the Environment

Agency, Health and Safety and our Derbyshire County and Parish Councils to do it. RASP says 'No.'"

"Steve Caddy from *The Sheffield Star*. John, what is your response to the threat that the police will make arrests if you continue to obstruct this company?"

"RASP's response to that is the real criminals are behind these gates, what they have done to the people of Killamarsh over the years is disgraceful. They have continually polluted and put the health and lives of the people of our village at risk. We don't want our members arrested, but if that's what it takes to shut down SARP UK, then so be it."

With this, the first of the police arrived, minus their mode of transport. SARP's workforce had already been trying to remove the chain and padlock for the best part of 20 minutes without success.

"Who has got the key?" asked a police officer.

We all looked round. The Grim Reaper had gone.

"Nobody here has the key," Colin Williams answered, and everyone from RASP knew he was telling the truth.

While the TV cameras whirred and the newspaper reporters wrote notes, RASP protesters chanted their anti-SARP songs. The SARP staff had to resort to bolt-cutters in an attempt to remove the chains: after another 30 minutes they finally removed them and the police formed a cordon to allow the tankers through, followed by the staff, who raced past the protesters into the company car park to much jeering and the call of, "You wont be going home early tonight."

That night the BBC and ITV both led with the same story, showing as always the two nitric acid leaks, then the protesters, the locked gates and tankers and staff unable to go into the plant. It made the front pages of all the local papers. We had done what we set out to do, disrupting this company, making life difficult for them, as they had done to us for so many years.

"When are we going to have a night out on our own?" It was Saturday June 20. Sandra's words had found me in the middle of writing a speech. I had been invited to Beighton on the coming Tuesday to talk to residents in the Beighton school.

I turned. "I don't know, I have so much to do."

"Do you know we have never been anywhere bar work and SARP for the best part of a month? We need to go out, just for a few hours."

As usual she was right. Ever since the leaks, our lives seemed to have been consumed by this campaign. "OK. We will go out for a meal tonight. I will ring and get a table at Bruce's."

That evening as we climbed the hill towards High Moor, still a part of Killamarsh, we passed the site of the old

High Moor colliery on the right, now overgrown with weeds and high grass, a sad reminder for lots of the ex-miners in our village of happier times when there were full wage packets on Friday nights. The road beyond High Moor is where the scenery changes very quickly, and you soon find yourself out in open countryside, heading out on the road towards Worksop and Sherwood Forest and the famous Welbeck estate of the Duke of Portland that stands in Clumber Park. We passed all this as we headed for Bruce's, otherwise known as the Mussel and Crab, Sandra's favourite restaurant, which lay just off the A1 on the Tuxford road, a beautiful part of North Nottinghamshire.

"It's lovely to get away for a few hours," were Sandra's words as she stared into her glass of Rioja.

We were about halfway through the meal when a party of eight at the next table started a conversation we could not help overhearing. "They are kicking up a right fuss over at Killamarsh."

"Yes," was the reply from a big guy at the top of the table. "They are wasting their time, they will never shut that incinerator, people been complaining for years. My daughter lives there."

The lady opposite him spoke up. "Well, if it was left to you, Eric, it would stay open. I admire that group RASP, I tell you they are not going to go down without a fight, good luck to them. They say that they are going to go to Paris to confront the owners."

As Killamarsh was the best part of 30 miles from this restaurant, I thought it was pretty good the word was spreading.

"We can't get away from SARP even when we come out here, can we?" said Sandra later when we sat down in the lounge area of the restaurant. I had been pleased to think that people were taking notice; I wasn't sure if Sandra was.

The meeting at the Crown was opened the following Monday as usual by Kevin Jones, who said to the packed room, "Once again the events of the last week have been remarkable, the protest at the gates on Thursday, the Grim Reaper locking the gates – by the way, who is that Grim Reaper…? We will pass on that, it was, as I say, remarkable, the television and newspaper coverage was brilliant. I'm going to hand over to Alistair to see what we have planned for the coming week."

"Yes, a great week, the pressure is really on SARP and this campaign is all about that, watching them for any errors, any leaks, and we know Leigh/SARP of old – they can't help themselves, the one thing you can rely on with them is that they will make errors, it's endemic in their culture. This coming week, John Moran is going to Beighton school to talk to the residents about our experiences in our village and to see if we can get Beighton residents to support RASP. Getting all the outside villages such as Mosborough, Beighton and Kiveton Park into the campaign is going to be very important. On a different topic, it has been suggested by many of you that if SARP's bosses will not come to see us, we should go to see them. That would mean going to Paris."

"I am up for that!" shouted May Hobson. May and Terry Hobson were in their sixties and lived on Nethermoor Lane, and had been in RASP since the beginning. Only small and slight was May, but like all the women in this group had that fearless attitude that many men in our community, although twice as big and strong, could not match.

"Yes, it looks like Paris. We would need to hire a coach, I don't know how much that would cost. Has anyone any ideas?" asked Alistair.

The one thing RASP always seemed to have was people with ideas and they always seemed to be original. The Grim Reaper, for example – nobody had ever used a Grim Reaper in a protest and I have no doubt that campaigns in the future will use one again.

"I know Alan Cooper pretty well, I will ask him how much it will cost," answered Steve Martin.

Alan Cooper ran a coach business based on the Norwood Industrial Estate, just behind my unit and very close to the SARP boundary fence. There was no love lost between Alan Cooper and SARP, that we already knew.

"How much do we have in the funds?" asked Kevin, turning to Samantha Martin.

"We have £346.56," was her reply.

"That's not bad, where have we collected that?" asked Ann Cockerill.

"Mainly at the public meetings and the protests – lots of people who don't want to come on the protests, but want to show their support," Samantha explained.

Alistair then continued. "I want to talk now about putting a 24-hour picket and watch on the gates at SARP, we must have a presence down there all the time. I know that some of you are there until midnight—" he looked in the direction of Ann Nettleship and her sister June Cullabine. It was true. Any night you went down to the gates of SARP, in rain or whatever weather, there were the two sisters sitting on the SARP wall waiting to stop tankers entering the site and talking to the drivers, asking them not to cross the picket line. Very occasionally one would not cross, which was a great success.

"We will do a shift timetable that will help June and Ann and also put the place under surveillance every night. Have we any volunteers?" asked Alistair, looking around the room.

Allison Sampson was the first to answer, "I will."

"So will I," answered Sandra, sitting at my side.

The Toxic Night Shift had been born. For the next 18 months, it would become one of the most powerful tools that RASP had against SARP UK.

Tuesday night found me at the Junior School in Beighton. I joined Dr. Jon Dale, a doctor from Bolsover near Chesterfield, who was an expert on industrial health problems caused by pollution from companies such as SARP UK, the Coalite Plant at Bolsover that had been the scene of many accidents with dioxins in the last few years and the Wingerworth Coking Plant at Chesterfield. The killing fields of North Derbyshire was how they would be described by another top expert on pollution, Dr. Dick van Steenis, but that was in the future. Tonight, alongside Jon Dale and myself, was Ken Fleet, representing Ken Coates' office.

I was introduced by David Milson, who had spoken at the last public meeting in Killamarsh. "John Moran, Press Officer for the RASP campaign group at Killamarsh."

The school was packed that night with young and old residents, all worried about the health of their families from the threat from SARP UK.

If anyone had told me a month before that I would be opening a meeting to so many people I would have been terrified, but that was then, this was now and the anger was greater than the fear. "I am here to talk about RASP, or to give its full title, Residents Against SARP Pollution. Why do we need RASP? To begin with, as some of you might know, I am the milkman in Killamarsh and deliver to 600 households in the village. Over the last 10 years I have heard lone voices everywhere. The lady on Primrose Close who is afraid to leave her windows open day or night for fears of the smells and toxic fumes from the SARP plant. The lady on North Crescent who wakes choking because of the toxic fumes from the SARP plant. The haulage driver who starts work at 2.30 am on the Norwood Industrial Estate and can't breathe with the air pollution from the SARP plant. The couple who live on Sheffield Road who have complained for years of the smells coming from their cellar from the SARP plant. Residents from one end to the other of Sheffield Road who are almost knocked over by the fumes from the grids with the smells from the SARP plant.

"In my own experience, my delivery lads and myself with handkerchiefs over our faces in the early hours to protect us from the air pollution from the SARP plant. So really, RASP formed itself – all those lone voices are now one, and make no mistake, they are really being heard. Relatives and friends from as far away as the Isle of Wight in the south to Newcastle in the north telephone home to talk about it – everyone knows what's going at the SARP plant.

"We have noticed that recently the girl on the Yorkshire ITV weather map has started mentioning Killamarsh – some may argue that they have only just begun to be able to see us since the virtual closure of the SARP plant. So that brings me to the aims of RASP – we want to get 10,000 people to sign our petition, starting here tonight. So much for tonight's aims: what are the future aims of RASP? That's easy to answer.

"No early warning systems at the SARP plant! No emergency systems at the SARP plant! No compromise at the SARP plant! SARP incinerator out of Killamarsh forever! Fresh air to breathe in Killamarsh!"

RASP supporters were on their feet. The whole room was standing. We had struck a chord. We would collect over 250 signatures that night – Beighton had joined us at Killamarsh in our fight against SARP UK.

Chapter Five

The Children March

On the following Monday at our weekly meeting at the Crown, Kevin Jones opened proceedings with a rundown of the current state of play.

"The meeting at Beighton went very well, and as a result David Milson is here tonight to report." David Milson had been one of the three people I saw delivering leaflets the day after the second leak – he was a resident of Beighton.

"I want to thank RASP for coming to our inaugural meeting last Tuesday. As a result we have formed a RASP branch in Beighton. 250 people have joined and we will be holding weekly meetings to keep everyone at Beighton informed. We will join you in future marches and protests against SARP UK." This was received with much applause.

"I will hand over to you," Kevin said, now turning to Alistair.

"Yes, another good week. Has anyone got any ideas what we should do next week?"

Ann Cockerill was the first to reply. "I think that it is time we involved the Sheffield Road Junior and Infant schools in the campaign; after all, it's for those children that the closure of this incinerator is the most important. We should stage a protest with their mums and dads one morning, prior to school so that it would not interrupt the school day too much."

"I think that's a great idea. The headmaster and the governors have been very quiet – they have never once shown RASP any support. It's time we confronted them to find out where they stand," joined in Brian Ashmore. He wanted to know where his former employers stood like the rest of us.

Alistair continued, "What day should we do it and at what time would be best?"

The opinion was that we should meet at the school about 8.15 am on Thursday and set off on the march to SARP at 8.30 am.

"I think it would be best if we spoke with the headmaster first and got his backing; they may join us or certain teachers may come along." The voice of David Parr sounded a note of caution. David had been in the previous protest group in 1986, and we knew he didn't like the way that RASP distanced itself from MP Harry Barnes and the local Council, but nevertheless his passion to get rid of SARP could not be doubted.

"Who is going to meet Mr. McLeavy, the headmaster?" asked Kevin.

"I will," I answered. I had never met the man, as when my three children attended the school it had been a Mr. Howdle, or Harry as he was known, respected by everyone.

"Well, I will get on with the leaflets, and then we can hand them out Wednesday morning before school. Can I have some volunteers?" asked Alistair. Carol Dye, Allison Sampson and the two Martin sisters were given the job.

The following morning I finished the round for about 8.30 am, returning home as all the children were arriving at both Infant and Junior schools. The Junior School was the one closest to SARP; they had about 500 pupils aged seven to 11. Opposite was the smaller Infant School with about 200 pupils. I went into the school reception area. "I have come to speak with the headmaster. John Moran, Press Officer for RASP."

"I know who you are, you can wait outside his office, he will see you shortly." The reply I felt was not the most friendly, but I sat outside his office wondering what his reaction to the march would be. I did not have to wait long before the door opened.

"What can I do for you and RASP?" he asked as he showed me to a chair overlooking his highly polished desk with neat piles of papers, all in their proper places.

"I have come on behalf of RASP to ask your permission to allow pupils, with their parents, to march on Thursday at

8.30 am to the gates of SARP. We by law have informed the police who will escort us to the gates and back to the school for about 9.30 am."

Mr. McLeavy pondered the question for a few seconds then replied, "No, most definitely no. There will be no children from this school on your protest and no member of staff either."

I was stunned by the reply. "Do you mean to say that after all the problems with Sniffer Patrols and all the incidents you will not support us; if not us, for the sake of all your pupils and the generations to come?"

Above: Brenda Hancock masks up, long before COVID-19, to get her point across about the poor air quality, especially at the Sheffield Road schools. These were located very close to the SARP UK plant, and a large percentage of their pupils used inhalers.

Right: Thomas Robinson on the march, July 2, 1998. RASP had a wide range of ages attending its protests, particularly at the 'Children's March'. One of RASP's central aims was always to make Killamarsh a safe place to live for future generations.

He left the question unanswered. He rose from his chair, crossed the floor and asked me to leave. We now knew where we stood. He was only probably repeating the Derbyshire Council Education line anyway. The march would go on, the children would protest. There would be nobody that would dictate to us over SARP; those days were long gone.

On the Wednesday morning at 8.30 am, as I made my way back down Sheffield Road to my house on Belklane Drive next to the school, across the road I could see Carol Dye, Allison Sampson and the two Martin girls handing out the leaflets.

I made my way over to them. "How's it going, Carol?"

"Great, I think that we should get plenty of support, more so the ones who live up here on the Norwood. How did it go with Mr. McLeavy?"

"Not very well. He told me he would not allow it, no children, no teachers would be allowed on any protest."

"We will bloody well see about that! Hypocritical, stupid man – can't he see it's for the children we are doing it more than anyone?"

"No, he didn't waste any time, he soon put me straight," I answered. I left the four RASP women still handing out the leaflets for the march to SARP on the following morning.

I arrived back from the round on the Thursday in good time. We had informed all the media and we were expecting a decent turnout of parents and children. The BBC Radio

Sheffield and Radio Hallam cars were already in place, as were the camera crews of ITV and the BBC, and all the local newspapers, including *The Yorkshire Post*.

"Do you know what McLeavy has done, John?" was the greeting I was met with from Carol Dye.

Whatever it was, the dropping of the prefix of Mr. in his name suggested it wasn't good.

"He sent a letter home with every child to tell their parents that anyone going on the protest would be marked absent and the parents would receive a letter from the Derbyshire Education Committee. I know that a few have come to me and said they were afraid of the consequences if they kept their child away from school."

An attractive young lady battled her way through the crowd to where Carol and I were standing. "I am from BBC Radio Sheffield." After asking our names, she started her report for the listeners. "We are here this morning outside the Sheffield Road schools in Killamarsh, I have with me John Moran and Carol Dye from RASP. Could you tell me, John, what is happening here today? There are lots of children with banners and placards."

"We are here today to march with our children and grandchildren to the gates of SARP UK. They want fresh air to breathe, that is their right, for their health now and in the future, at these two schools. We cannot put a price on that."

Turning to Carol the reporter said, "We now speak to mum of two Carol Dye. Carol, are you marching with your children today?"

"Yes, I certainly am, my children both have inhalers, as do most of the children who attend these schools. We don't want Sniffer Patrols at breaktime, we want them to play out without the fear of SARP sending over their dioxins and toxic clouds."

"How many children are you expecting to be on the march?" She turned her mike towards me.

"I would say 50 children and their parents will join us on the march to the gates of SARP UK. It would have been a lot more, but the school have threatened that all children on the march will be marked absent and will receive a letter from the Derbyshire Education Committee and the school governors."

"What is RASP's response to that?" she asked.

"Our response at RASP is that we march and I am proud of the parents who have not been intimidated by the school's threats. RASP is trying to close and remove this incinerator on its own – we have no backing from the Parish, District and County Councils, they are never with us on our protests and we feel that the Derbyshire County Council does not have the same desire, for whatever reason, to close this company down."

The time was now just before 8.30 am. Carol, with her two children, one in each hand, walked with me to the head of the protest. The Martin girls, holding their RASP banner high, walked in front of us. The march had only gone a few yards when from a little snicket (a Derbyshire word for path) emerged the Grim Reaper, scythe in hand.

We moved more slowly than on a normal march. The police outriders on motorbikes had to keep stopping as little legs hurried to keep up, mums with prams like Tony Ward's daughter with ten-month-old Thomas Robinson holding a plaque which read "LET ME BREATHE! SHUT DOWN SARP," Brenda Hancock with a white medical mask covering the lower half of her face, Brian Ashmore with a small wooden cross with the words "SARP OUT" across the top, wearing his familiar black beret.

"CLOSE DOWN SARP." The message to SARP was everywhere. There is nothing more emotive than small children marching. Motorists stopped or slowed down, honking their car horns in support. We marched to the gates of SARP and stood outside with the children. The TV and all the media followed, cameras whirring. We then marched back to the school, returning at about 9.30 am. I can say how proud we were at RASP that day of the mums and children who had defied the authorities who had tried to intimidate them.

That evening's front page of *The Sheffield Star* had a half-page picture of Thomas Robinson in his pram holding his placard with the headline, "Kids Lead Fight on Waste Plant." On page three was another half-page picture, this one of Brenda Hancock in her white mask holding a placard proclaiming, "SAY NO TO TOXIC WASTE" with the headline across the page, "March Against Poison Gas Plant." Both the TV channels carried the story in their regional news bulletins, with footage of the children marching.

In the morning *The Yorkshire Post* had the headline "School Sniffer Patrols Denied". The report read: "A school has denied it has 'Sniffer Patrols' to detect nasty whiffs from a nearby chemical plant. The headmaster, David McLeavy, said, 'We are not constantly sniffing the air, we are not constantly patrolling or bringing the children into school.' John Moran, from Residents Against SARP Pollution (RASP), said dinner ladies had been instructed by senior members of staff to bring children inside if they could smell anything suspicious. He said, 'It's like a Sniffer Patrol – it's a well-known fact.'"

That Saturday I had just finished the round, when I called in at the Post Office on Bridge Street to send in my welfare tokens for redemption. These were what entitled people on low incomes to have seven pints of milk free per week, and I always called in each Saturday to post them off. Something caught my eye in the window as I was leaving.

Let not historians one day show

An area where no things grow.

Bereft it seems of living thing,

Where still the air and no birds sing.

No sound of happy children playing,

No eager footsteps o'er fields straying,

No sound of laughter – nor of weeping,

For those who did are long time sleeping.

Let no one ponder on the fate

Of this place now so desolate

Marked by a plinth, with letters harsh

Here was a spot called Killamarsh.

TUP

It was Monday morning. The alarm had just gone off at 2.50 am, although I hardly needed it after 22 years, first for Express Dairy in Sheffield and for the last nine in Killamarsh. I thought I would go down a few minutes early to the unit on the Norwood Industrial Estate to see how the Toxic Night Shift was coping. I drove down through the wet, rainy night, SARP's office lights reflecting off Ellisons Road, SARP's own site lights trying to break through the permanent shroud of mist that always enveloped this place, where that obnoxious smell of sickly plastic permanently pervaded the air. There in the gloom, on the SARP wall, sat Allison Sampson and my wife Sandra.

"I've brought you some coffee, thought you might need it." I handed over the flask I had brought from home. "How's it going?"

"It has been pretty quiet, not as many tankers coming in. Only one of the seven processes has been restarted, might be different when they restart the others," was Allison's reply.

Sandra had come here straight from work at about 11.00 pm, when she and Allison had taken over from Ann Nettleship and her sister June Cullabine.

"There was plenty going on when we got here, Ann and June had called the Environment Agency on their 24-hour hotline, so two inspectors were down because of the foul smells that were coming from the site, they were very bad about 11.00 pm. Do you know we have had them out every night for the last two weeks?" Allison said with a twinkle in her eye.

"When is your shift over?" I asked.

"I will be home in about half an hour, Ann Cockerill and Margaret Ashmore will take over until 7.30 am," were Sandra's parting words as I slowly moved off to start my morning deliveries.

The meeting was opened as usual by Kevin Jones at the Crown on the following Monday. "Well done to everyone on the march with the children, the media coverage we received was unbelievable. The front page of *The Sheffield Star*, TV and radio... it seems we are on every news bulletin throughout the day. Alistair, I will hand over to you to bring us up to date about what we are planning next week."

"The trip to Paris is planned for Thursday July 23. Alan Cooper has provided us with two coaches at very little cost, with two drivers on each. We will set off at 9.00 pm on the Thursday, returning back home at about 6.00 am on the Saturday morning. We are putting a cost of around £30 – anything we have over will go back into RASP's funds. We will put posters up round the village for anyone who wants to come, Julie Martin is organising the trip and she is the one anyone wishing to go must contact.

"The Toxic Night Shift is having an effect; I have heard the EA are complaining to the Council about the number of times we have had them out to the site over the last few weeks, but have admitted that in every case the smells are unacceptable, that the smells should not pass beyond the site boundaries – a statement that beggars belief after what they have allowed over the last 20 years. We are also arranging a public meeting at the Village Centre in Killamarsh for Tuesday July 14 at 7.45 pm. We have had these yellow leaflets printed and we have to deliver them to every household in the village – you can collect 100 each from Trevor Cockerill and arrange what roads you will cover so we are not delivering to the same houses twice. We will put them on all the lampposts and shops in the village. This is publicising a meeting called by RASP to update the Killamarsh public as to where we have reached in our campaign."

In the following days, yellow RASP posters seemed to be everywhere, on every lamppost and in most of the shops. There would be no one who didn't know RASP was holding its first public meeting.

It had been just six weeks since the start of the campaign. Many things had happened, RASP had been formed, protests organised, TV and press coverage every day. Most people in the village had chosen where they stood and the majority were with us, but there were people and families who were employed at the site and its closure would mean the inevitable loss of jobs. It was about this time that I noticed that I was beginning to lose customers on the milk round. The customers lost mostly had links to SARP UK; they had been customers to me over many years, but now the battle lines had been drawn.

In the past when I lost a customer in the village I would always make a point of visiting them at the first opportunity to try to sort out any problem they might have with the delivery. Now I didn't have to try – there was no middle ground. As someone in RASP once said, "It's them or us."

The phone rang about 11.00 am on Thursday. It was Alistair. "Tomorrow, John, I am arranging another protest, early morning. The Toxic Night Shift has reported that they open the gates about 6.30 am and they then clear off for breakfast leaving the whole site without security. I think that we should do something to expose this."

"What did you have in mind?" I asked.

"Well, we will go through the gates of the site if we get a chance. We will probably face arrest for trespass. I will put that to the protesters when we are about to march," he added.

The following morning we assembled near my cold storage unit, intending to take the same route as we had on the protest when the Grim Reaper had padlocked the gates. The time was 6.45 am. Alistair, turning to the 50 RASP protesters who stood behind him, explained, "We plan to enter the site if the gates have been left open. Anyone who does not feel comfortable with that, wait at the gates and continue your protest there."

With that we moved, more like a guerrilla army than milkmen, dinner ladies, care workers, publicans and pensioners. We turned the corner; SARP lay ahead on the left. On the right we passed Alan Cooper's coach depot, from which would be supplied RASP's transport to the Paris protest a couple of weeks later. The security man Tony Milner watched in amazement as this ragtag army passed. Tony was unkindly known as the Hobby Bobby for his role as special constable in the village, but in fact he was like the Toxic Night Shift, the nocturnal eyes of RASP – nothing ever went unseen.

"Morning, Tony," we mouthed as we passed him, not wanting to announce our arrival to SARP just yet. When we got there the gates were indeed wide open – the Toxic Night Shift had got it right once again.

We all followed the Grim Reaper and Alistair as they walked through the main gates. There was not a soul to stop us as we walked around SARP's administration block. Looking back, I saw with pride that not one of the 50 protesters had stopped at the gates. We entered the reception area of the main block and left placards reading, "SARP Out!" "No Toxic Waste" against the windows and doors. We then marched back to the gates, but not before the media had arrived.

The BBC Radio Sheffield reporter was the first on the scene. I heard him say, "We are outside the SARP UK chemical plant at Killamarsh, the scene of many protests by the campaign group RASP over the last months. We are going to speak to John Moran, the Press Officer of RASP. You have just been seen to be trespassing all over this site. Can you tell me for what purpose you have done this and why you left your placards and banners all over the office block?"

"We are here today to show the appalling security in place at this chemical waste plant. This is one of the four most dangerous chemical waste plants in the UK, in fact, because of the condition of the place it is *the* most dangerous. That anyone can walk in unchallenged shows what a shambles of a company this is."

"All of you risked being arrested for trespass this morning, what will you say if that happens?"

"We all know the risk of arrests. Our concern is, what are the risks that this plant are taking with the lives and health of the people of our village?"

His closing words were, "With that I return you to the studio from Killamarsh after an amazing breach of security at this controversial chemical waste reprocessing plant."

Once again that night, on every regional news report we were seen marching around the administration block. The media attack we were launching on this company was incessant. They were error-prone and for every error they made, we would be waiting and watching, 24 hours a day.

The final twist to the walk around the admin block was when the Grim Reaper padlocked the gates once again and someone left a big placard reading, "Last One Out Please Lock Up."

Chapter Six

The Sainsbury's Carrier Bag and the Toxic Ship

It was Friday night. I turned to Sandra, who had just returned from her afternoon shift at Derwent House, the care home she worked at for the Derbyshire County Council in Newbold, Chesterfield.

"I fancy a run-out tomorrow. I think we will go up to Whitby, what do you think?"

"That would be lovely," she answered. A visit to Whitby meant only one thing – as Rick Stein once famously said, "The best fish and chip shop in the world, the Magpie."

The next day we were on our way to Whitby. We had gone with our friends Ann and Trevor Cockerill. Trevor always drove even though he drove as part of his job for the printing company he worked for. He always seemed to enjoy driving and I didn't mind at all; he was one of the few people with whom I could relax when not driving.

It was mid afternoon when we arrived in Whitby. It has always been one of my favourite places, set in the beautiful countryside made famous by the TV series *Heartbeat*. We parked up on the outskirts of the town – devil of a place to park, Whitby – and spent a lovely hour or two walking around. At about 5.00 pm we headed for the Magpie, a black and white building with two magpies painted on the front wall. It was right next to the quayside from which three times a day the Magpie had its fresh catch delivered. We joined the inevitable queue of people that always seemed to be waiting outside, and finally we were found a table.

"No need to look at the menu, I know what I am having," said Sandra, the Magpie's fried halibut being her obvious favourite. Soon four halibut were being devoured, accompanied by a nice bottle of chilled Chablis.

"That's as good as it gets for a Yorkshireman. Fish and chips at Whitby on a summer's afternoon," Trevor commented as he finished his meal.

"Simple souls, these Yorkshiremen," I teased. He knew full well that I was a Lancastrian, originally from Manchester.

We left the Magpie and wandered down the old streets. We were passing a newspaper shop when we noticed on the news board outside the words, "Orange Balloons Land in

Whitby". The local newspaper confirmed the story of how orange balloons from a place called Killamarsh had been found in the gardens of people in Whitby. The distance from Killamarsh to Whitby being around 85 miles, the conclusion was that nitric acid clouds travel a long way; so it would seem does the name of RASP.

We arrived back home around 11.30 pm that Saturday night. We had enjoyed the break from constant campaigning. Trevor and Ann, like ourselves, had been on every protest and march; they were as tired as we were, but like all at RASP they put it out of their minds and concentrated on the campaign.

The following day, Sunday, was my only day off from the milk round. With no early start at 3.00 am, I always enjoyed the lie-in, which was usually until about 8.00 am. However, on this Sunday it was about 5.00 am when something disturbed me. I could have sworn I heard my gate being closed, so I got up and went to the window that overlooked my front gate. All was quiet. I could not see down Belklane Drive because we had a very thick conifer hedge, but there didn't seem to be a soul about. I went back to bed and around 8.30 am I awoke again and decided to go down and make a morning coffee. Sandra was never at her best first thing in the morning, so I always let her have a lie-in before waking her about 9.30 am with a cup of tea. The thought of the closing gate was the furthest thing from my mind as I opened the door that Sunday morning to let our Yorkshire terriers out.

There on the step was a Sainsbury's carrier bag.

I knew that there had been nothing on the step when I had come in the night before. The bag appeared to be full, and when I bent down to look I saw it was stuffed with what appeared to be files and documents. It also had one of our yellow RASP public meeting posters taped to the side, on which words had been added with marker pen, each letter different as if the person did not want their writing to be identified.

LEIGH =SARP
SAME PLANT
SAME EMPLOYEES
SAME DIRECTORS
SAME FAULTS
SAME LIES
SAME DANGERS.

Intrigued to know what was inside, I closed the front door behind me and took the bag to my study. I carefully took a huge wad of documents out and laid them on the desk. Many thoughts were racing through my head. Who could have left them? When could they have left them? Why had they left them? Then I remembered the closing gate, Whoever left them had come in the middle of the night, dropped them on the doorstep and disappeared as quickly as they had come.

It was a treasure trove. In the bag were internal memos, internal site reports and contracts covering the last 12 years at Leigh/SARP UK. There was no clue left to the person who had brought them that Sunday morning in July. His or her identity remains RASP's greatest mystery, but to that person we at RASP will always owe a deep debt of gratitude.

I started to look through what had been left; there was so much to read and digest, but I knew what we had in those documents confirmed what we had all at RASP feared all these years, but up to now all we had ever got was denials.

Sandra came down about 9.30 am.

"You are not going to believe what was left on our step in the night," I told her. She didn't have to guess, as I was surrounded by all the files and documents.

"Who could have left them?" was all she could say.

"I don't know, I haven't a clue, but someone who wasn't very happy with the way they do things."

Over the next couple of days I spent every available minute studying all the reports, files and contract information in the papers. The only time I was not doing so was when I was out delivering and while I was at the Monday night meeting at the Crown. That Monday, Kevin Jones was away on business and could not attend. Wendy Wellings was made Chairperson for the night, and sitting alongside Wendy was her daughter Louise.

Wendy began, "In the absence of Kevin I am opening the meeting by saying that I expect everyone has seen the local papers reporting on the orange balloons being found as far away as Whitby."

Everyone nodded. Every paper, every radio news report and every television visit to Killamarsh and the SARP plant were never missed.

"Alistair, can you bring us up to date with future plans?" Wendy handed over the floor to Alistair.

"The coaches for Paris are filling up well. We still have a few seats available, so if you know anyone who would like to come with us, ask them to contact Samantha Martin. Tomorrow night we have the RASP public meeting at the Killamarsh Leisure Centre at 7.45 pm. I hope you all can make it. We also have a Community Inquiry on July 25 – that is the Saturday we get back from Paris – at 11.00 am at the St. Giles Church Hall on Sheepcote Road. It's being chaired by Ken Coates MEP, with a panel including Dr. William R. Gray of Eckington, Dr. Jon Dale of Bolsover and Hugh Ellis of the Coalfield Planning Co-op. Lastly, we have been working on a RASP newsletter. We will give more details next week and we hope to bring one out every two weeks, there is enough going on every week, I don't think we will have any difficulty filling one fortnightly. That is about all that there is."

"Thank you, Alistair, I would say that was plenty for us to think about." Wendy, turning to me, asked, "John, have you anything to report?"

"No, not much." I was wanting to tell them all about the Sainsbury's carrier bag and the early morning caller, but needed more time to go through all the papers, and with the RASP public meeting coming up on the next night, that would be as good as time as any to tell them.

I spent all of Tuesday digesting as much information as I could, making notes. I knew this speech to RASP was going to last a long time.

On Tuesday night the Leisure Centre was filling up fast, with almost as many people as when the Killamarsh Council had held a public meeting here. Many familiar faces were in the front few rows, including Ann and Trevor Cockerill with Kevin and Allison Sampson alongside them. On the second row were Ann Nettleship and her sister June Cullabine next to Tony Ward and his wife Ann, whose grandson Thomas Robinson had appeared on the front page of *The Sheffield Star* in his pram in the children's march on SARP UK. Next to them was Sandra and my daughter Faye, Myra and Terry Turner, Brenda Glossop, Pat Whitehouse, David Milson and

Alistair. It was Alistair's decision not to be on the platform, as he felt that the Parish Council would condemn RASP for having connections politically with the Socialist Party. In truth, the Socialist Party and Ken Coates' office at Chesterfield were the only friends that RASP had throughout the campaign. At no time in all of the campaign had Alistair tried to persuade anyone to join the Socialist Party; in fact, apart from one person, no one ever did.

Kevin Jones opened the meeting, flanked by me to his left and Roger Barraclough to his right. Kevin turned to Roger and myself and said quietly so no one could hear, "I hope you two have something to keep them interested; we have got the room booked till 10.30."

"Don't worry, Kevin, I'm sure there will be plenty to talk about," was my reply.

He introduced himself to the audience. Most knew him but there were lots of faces from the village we did not recognise. I did notice that all the Parish Councillors were sitting on the back row.

"I am Kevin Jones, the Chairman of RASP, and I would like to introduce Roger Barraclough, our Vice-Chairman, and John Moran, our Press Officer. First I would like Roger to tell us the story so far."

"Residents Against SARP Pollution, or RASP as we are known, was set up after the public meetings and mass protests after two toxic gas leaks at the SARP UK Killamarsh Chemical Waste Plant. Residents from Killamarsh and neighbouring villages and townships are campaigning to get SARP closed down and relocated away from populated areas, We do not believe it is possible to make the site 100 percent safe and therefore it is unacceptable to process potentially lethal substances in residential areas, let alone 100 yards from the school playing fields next to the Rother Valley Country Park. Formerly Leigh Environmental, it is now part of the huge French multinational called Vivendi, which is currently promoting itself as 'environmentally friendly'. Management say their first priority is safety, yet now they have restarted some processes without even the most basic emergency or warning systems in place. Profits before people, one can only assume. These bosses don't live locally and don't have to suffer the constant emissions and smells, nor the dangers of a third potentially lethal accident. RASP will not stop campaigning until SARP is closed and we don't have to live with this threat any more. Over 1,000 residents marched on SARP UK on Saturday June 13 in a huge show of people power. We have gained the support of many, including Mr. Ken Coates MEP and Mr. Alan Charles, our Derbyshire County Councillor, and others. An action committee has now been set up to organise future protests and campaigning activities. We have a petition that asks for the closure of SARP UK and would ask you to sign that petition before you leave tonight. The forms are available at the desk at the exit. Thank you."

He sat down to loud applause from the audience, mainly RASP and not so much the Parish Council, who looked quite unmoved by Roger's offering. Maybe I could get some reaction when they had heard what I had to say.

Kevin then turned to me. "And now the Press Officer for RASP, John Moran, has something he would like to say."

As I rose to my feet and looked out across the packed room I saw that the TV crews and reporters from all the newspapers were there, two cameramen stationed at the front on either side.

"Thank you, everyone, for coming to this first RASP public meeting. There were many things I wanted to talk about this evening about the battle we are having with this company, but I am afraid that will have to wait for another time, another RASP meeting. On Sunday morning, I had a visitor in the early hours. He or she never knocked, never left their name. What they did leave was a Sainsbury's carrier bag on my doorstep. Tonight I am going to talk about what was in that bag." I lifted the carrier bag onto the table, removed the yellow RASP poster from the side, and held it up to show the audience before reading it aloud.

"LEIGH=SARP

SAME PLANT

SAME EMPLOYEES

SAME DIRECTORS
SAME FAULTS
SAME LIES
SAME DANGERS."

"This was the contents of that bag." I lifted the pile of files and document in the air. "These are internal memos, site reports and inspections of tanks at Leigh/SARP UK over the last 12 years."

There was a hush from the packed audience. Only Sandra and I, and of course one other unknown person, knew what had been left. Was that person in the room that night?

"I will show you tonight why we protest against Leigh/SARP, why we are right to, why the dangers we face from this company are very real. I will show a waste plant falling apart, with old, decaying storage tanks, a highly dangerous second-hand incinerator, appalling work practices and, most worryingly, a collusion between Leigh/SARP and the people who are supposed to protect us."

I looked down, picking up the top files and began to read, "Subject: Site Visit to Killamarsh. 'The condition of the site overall was found to be extremely disappointing. It is appreciated that major works are in progress concerning the removal of tanks which are no longer serviceable and soil. In some areas, quarrying materials are being laid down and none of these operations are conducive to achieving a clean and tidy operation. However, there are degrees, and it is felt that in some areas mud at least 12 inches deep is totally inappropriate. Acid Treatment Plant: The redundant tanks adjacent to the acid storage/treatment tanks have been removed and this area is in need of tidying to remove old concrete and debris. The acid treatment/storage tanks were perilously close to overflowing and level devices should be fitted to ensure adequate leeway. There was evidence during a later visit the same day that liquors had indeed spilled and were running in the direction of the lagoon.

"'Reports re: State and Contents of Storage Tanks. These tanks are in continuous use; they look OK but we have never had the metal tested for thickness. They are believed to be approximately 40 to 50 years old.'" I reminded everyone that it was one of these storage tanks that had split apart in the second explosion on May 30 this year, then continued reading. "Incineration Plant. The unit itself is much too close to the heat exchanger chambers, and we are suffering very bad flame impingement onto the heat exchanger tubes. At the moment we have written off two banks of tubes at a cost of £2,000 per bank. An additional point, which luckily has not been picked up by the authorities, is with the position of unit one, where the flames are basically being cooled immediately they leave the incinerator. This is actually cutting down the retention time from what is required, and is certainly illegal.

"'Site in General. When Mr. O'Connor did his site audit, which I believe was in September time, he said in his report at the time that one corner of the bund wall was starting to weep into the county dyke. The slow weep on one corner has turned into a now measurable flow. This could do with being chased at every level, as we would be in very serious legal problems if it got noticed by the National Rivers Authority.

"'Drum Storage. There are an excessive number of drums stored outside the laboratory and adjacent to the car park and below the industrial cleaning divisions area. Chlorinated solvents were stored in close proximity to highly flammable solvents, a highly dangerous practise generally frowned upon.

"'Field Sludge Area. We now have the new holder in place but the tanks in the field are most definitely illegal if the factory inspector were to see them.'" I took a sip of water and continued. "There is a Ciba-Geigy [chemicals multinational] audit of the site. Its conclusion was, 'The general overview of the site and Leigh as a company was taken into account when making the decision not to use this site. Ground Water Pollution. Their belief is that since some of the drum emptying operations for incineration, solvent recovery, bulking etc. takes place on unmade ground, spillages occur. This leads to ground contamination which could lead to groundwater pollution. Their opinion is that we do not know the hydrological condition of our site and thus may be unaware of groundwater problems occurring several miles away due entirely to our site operations.'"

Taking another sip of water from the glass on the table, I continued, "So that was the state of the site on one visit. What about the people who have done business with this company – what do they think about the Killamarsh operation? I have here a letter to this company from Rechem Waste Services about a flatbed vehicle from the Killamarsh site. 'I was on site at Pontypool when the above vehicle from your Killamarsh plant delivering capacitors was being offloaded. I was asked to look at the load because of the appalling condition it was in and I was shown photographs which had been taken before the offloading commenced. At the time when I inspected the vehicle only a small number of capacitors and cardboard kegs remained on the vehicle, and our staff, together with your driver, were still spreading sawdust onto the vehicle in order to mop up the liquid PCBs which were standing on the boards. The only items which were strapped down during transit were the kegs. None of the capacitors were strapped down in any way. Most were unwrapped, but some were wrapped in polythene and although the vehicle was sheeted in it, it is amazing that none of these capacitors fell off during transit. The main problem with the load, however, was the large number of capacitors which had some of their ceramic connectors broken off, thereby allowing PCBs to escape, and although attempts had been made to plug these holes with ill-fitting crude wooden plugs (the wooden plugs looked like sticks of firelighter), the PCBs were liberally escaping. Some of the capacitors had substantial holes in the body and some were so corroded that the seams were also leaking. The whole affair was such a mess that when the vehicle arrived, PCBs were dripping freely through the trailer down the sides. Never in my life have I personally witnessed such an appalling state of affairs and I am only thankful that this situation was not witnessed by any of the local authorities or local people, as it would not have been you who would have to take the brunt of the PR attack which would follow but ourselves. Road transport of toxic waste in Gwent is particularly sensitive at the moment, with the County Council calling for the Welsh office to conduct an inquiry into the situation, and it is being used as a further means of attack against Rechem, as current tactics are not proving successful for the protesting groups and hence fears of an incident involving the transport of hazardous wastes are being fired up. I understand, and again we have photographs to show the situation, that this is the second load to arrive from your plant in this sort of condition and neither management, nor the workforce at Pontypool, is prepared to allow this situation to occur a third time. Therefore, I must inform you that should you require to use our facilities for the destruction of capacitors or any other PCB-contaminated material in the future we will only be prepared to accept the waste on the basis that it is delivered on our own vehicle after being loaded under our supervision. I can assure you that if this load had been a Rechem load the person or persons responsible for its state would have been instantly dismissed, but what action you consider necessary is up to you. I think it is also worth mentioning that our Pontypool plant has just received a visit from three of your colleagues from your Brownhills site as a result of a third appalling load of mixed chemicals and I feel that you should be aware that unless your company can sort out these problems then our people will in the future refuse to handle any waste from your company.'"

I finished by showing the letter to the audience with a recently added black marker pen addition, "STILL EMPLOYED BY SARP UK NOW." Caught up in my speech, I did not notice that by this point several of the women in the audience, Ann Cockerill in particular, had tears streaming down their faces. Sandra told me later of their reaction – the revelations had obviously touched a chord and they were all very angry.

I then placed the letter from Rechem on the table and picked up another. "The next letter is from Derbyshire County Council Land and Building Subcommittee regarding the fire and explosion back in 1986. '(1) On September 10 1986 a fire occurred at the premises of Leigh Environmental at Killamarsh involving an aerosol destruction unit which was housed in a steel-framed asbestos-clad building, As yet it is unclear how the fire started and both the Fire Officer and the Factory Inspector are undertaking further investigations. (2) During the incidents a large number of aerosol cans of household products such as polish and air freshener exploded and were projected out of the building. In addition, because of the proximity of a large diesel tank and a waste chemical store, householders in the vicinity and occupants of the local school were advised to stay indoors until the fire could be brought under control.'

"You will please be aware that in this letter they fail to mention that the large diesel tank contained full capacitors of PCBs that can only be incinerated at places like Rechem at Pontypool because of the high-temperature incineration required. They only described it as a tank full of diesel. No mention of the PCBs that give off some of the most dangerous cancer-giving dioxins known to man. Clipped to the letter was a company newsletter from Leigh, it read 'Tests for dioxins and furans, the toxic thermal breakdowns of polychlorinated biphenyls (PCBs), are being carried out in soil near the Killamarsh Sheffield waste treatment facility operated by Leigh Environmental following a serious explosion of decontaminating PCB capacitors. The incident on September 10 occurred when an aerosol-crushing plant which had been brought into the building ignited. The fire spread to 700 gallons of diesel oil containing PCBs from the capacitor decontamination operations, which had been conducted in the adjacent plant.' Our Derbyshire County Council, the Fire Officer and the Factory Inspector (Health and Safety) were either unaware of the contents of the diesel tank or chose to omit it from their report in the face of what would have been a huge public awareness of what dangers came from this site."

The ship from another planet. The Karin B spent months at sea having been rejected from port after port, but our village of Killamarsh came close to being the final destination for her highly toxic cargo.

(Pictured at Brunsbuttel, Northern Germany, February 6, 2007, photo by Olaf Kuhnke, shipspotting.com)

I had now been talking for what seemed a long time, but it was probably about 40 minutes. I thanked my audience for their patience, but in reality you could have heard a pin drop all the time I was speaking. I took what was to be my final drink of water that night and continued.

"Tonight I want to tell you a story. Some with long memories might remember back to 1988, when we in this village were all aware of a ship called the *Karin B*. To most people the voyage of the *Karin B* was remarkable. Ships carrying 2,000 tonnes of badly packaged industrial solvents do not usually take to the seas with an unknown destination. The story begins on a beach near Koko in Nigeria. Two students visiting the area noticed drums of toxic waste marked with skulls and crossbones leaking into the pools where local people fetched their fresh water from and where their children played. The students alerted the environmental organisation Friends of the Earth in London, who sent two of their people to investigate. They concluded that up to 50 percent of the drums and containers were in appalling physical condition, many clearly leaking or had burst, and contained pesticides, PCBs plus chlorinated hydrocarbons, which require sophisticated incineration. The toxic waste had been illegally deposited in Nigeria, it appeared by an Italian construction company. Having set up a waste disposal company, they won the contract from the Italian government to dispose of the waste, a contract worth millions of lire. The company hired a boat, loaded the toxic waste onto it and took it to Nigeria, where they offloaded it at Koko after paying a local facilitator. Due to the international outcry after the visit from Friends of the Earth, the Italian government chartered the *Karin B* to go to Koko and retrieve the toxic waste. This is how the *Karin B* ended up on the high seas with no known destination. On July 27, after a three-day stop at Las Palmas, Canary Islands, and having been escorted away from Cadiz on mainland Spain by gunboats, the *Karin B* found herself off the coast of France. Here too her attempts to land her cargo were met with an armed vessel, this time from the French navy. The *Karin B* sailed to the Netherlands, who, having been forewarned, were waiting with a similar reception. The toxic ship next appeared off the Welsh coast on July 30. John Cunningham, the Shadow Environment Secretary, suggested that she was 'secretly and surreptitiously' invited into British waters by an unknown waste contractor. In the UK at this time, only Rechem at Pontypool had an incinerator capable of dealing with such a dangerous toxic cargo."

The press at the time had described the *Karin B* as the "ship from another planet", and to quote an article by Tyler Marshall in the *Los Angeles Times* of February 1999, "The *Karin B* is a small ship, but its odyssey stirred a continent."

"The *Karin B* sailed on and was last seen off Barrow-in-Furness on the north-west coast of Cumbria. That is where Killamarsh comes into the story. Until now, we never knew for sure that it was heading our way, down Ellisons Road, where outside these gates you can hear the sound of the children at the Sheffield Road schools as they play, unaware of the danger so close by at this plant." Turning to my audience, I held up the white faxed telegram in my outstretched hand. "Here is the proof."

I placed the telegram down on the table and with my left hand picked up letters from the Italian-owned company Ambiente acting on behalf of the Italian government for its disposal of the cargo of the *Karin B*. With my right hand I picked up a ten-page estimate handwritten in pen and ink by Leigh for the disposal of the toxic cargo. Facing the audience I said, "The total sum of £643,780. That was not the true price of bringing the toxic cargo through our village, down Ellisons Road, a cargo that no one else in Europe wanted. The true cost would have been, but for the grace of God, the health and safety of everyone in our village. The worrying thing for us all is how many other toxic cargoes have got through to be incinerated in a second-hand incinerator that was completely inadequate for the burning of such toxic substances?"

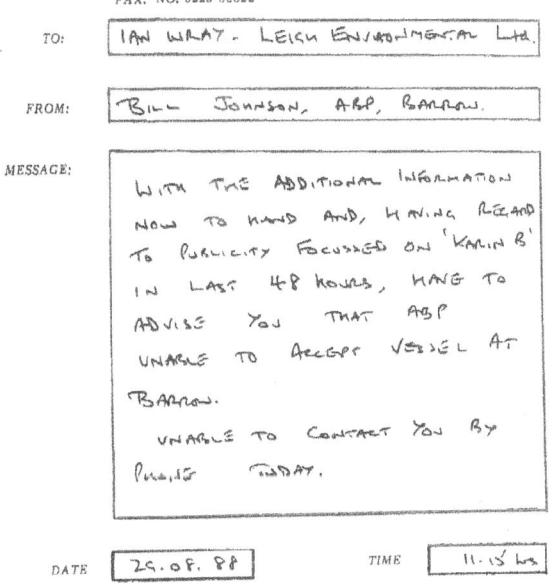

Communication between Leigh Environmental and the Italian company who were responsible for disposal of the Karin B's *toxic cargo continued, as Ambiente desperately searched for a solution. In the meantime, the ship's crew were getting sick from proximity to the chemicals, and we in Killamarsh were increasingly troubled by rumours that this sword of Damocles was hanging over us.*

The cost. Leigh Environmental's handwritten estimate of what they would charge to receive and dispose of the Karin B*'s cargo. The eventual cost of its proper disposal in Italy would prove to be in the millions, suggesting that Leigh would have conducted this dangerous business "on the cheap" in our backyard.*

Ambiente

Società per azioni con sede in Roma
P.le Enrico Mattei, 1 - 00144 Roma
Capitale Sociale L. 4.000.000.000 int. versato

Trib. di Roma Reg. Soc. n. 7200/87
C.C.I.A.A. Roma 638307
Part.Iva IVA e Codice Fiscale 07999260586

uffici
Via Paisiello Donci 273 - 00143 Roma
Tel. 06/8441 554 - Tx 610620 - Telefax 06/5441544

Via A. De Gasperi 16 - 20097 San Donato Milanese
Tel. 02/520 5989 - Tx 310246 - Telefax 02/5209639

riferimenti da citare nella risposta
emittente   protocollo
MP/mt   N.   1264

S. Donato Milanese,   7.9.1988

Messrs.
IAN WRAY
Leigh Environmental Ltd
Killamarsh, Sheffield
U.K.

RE : Industrial Toxic Wastes on Karin "B" and Deep Sea Carrier

We are interested in receiving your price list for final disposal of the captioned wastes detailed in the attachment "estimate composition and quantity of waste".

We realize that for a proper evaluation you need the analysis per each drum but, as you know, it will be available only later on.

For the time being, we are asking you to submit a list of prices covering the range of wastes that, according to your experience and based on the enclosed "estimate", we will have to dispose.

- delivery of wastes   : at your works (pls specify location)
- package of wastes   : in drums with detailed analysis
- timing   : please specify your expected time for disposal
- other conditions   : please specify, if any
- terms of payment   : please specify

Hoping to receive your offer ASAP, we remain at your disposal for any additional information you may need.

Contact person   : Carlo Pasini   (02-5205989) or
                    Mario Pomponio (02-5205537)
                    tlx 310246 ENI for AMBIENTE SPA
                    Fax (02-52022379)

Regards
M. Pomponio

I had been on the platform for the best part of an hour and a quarter. I had almost lost my voice, but not my sight. The Parish and District Councillors were running for the doors – we all knew their weakness had almost cost us dear. All hell broke loose among those who stayed in the room, with TV reporters and journalists ringing their bosses asking if they could cover the story; they were frightened of the legal repercussions because of the sensitivity of the internal memos and files and how they had been obtained.

After two months, the ordeal of the *Karin B* ended in Livorno, Italy. This was not before several of the crew reported feeling chest pains as a result of weeks spent at sea in close proximity to the toxic cargo. In a remote corner of the sprawling industrial port, specialists working in oxygen masks and protective clothing carefully repackaged the ship's cargo of 14,000 drums and assorted debris. Unloading cost £8 million. How could Leigh have considered doing it for £643,780?

The following Saturday, after finishing my round at about 9.30 am, I made my usual stop at the Post Office in Bridge Street to post my milk welfare tokens. On coming out, I looked to the window as I now always did, just in case 'Owd Tup' had called. Sure enough, there was a new poem.

Mother, what is that orange cloud there, making all the sky go dark?

Should it really be allowed there, over Rother Valley Park?

Mother, why are no birds singing? Silent the blackbird, thrush and lark.

Why the geese so swiftly winging far from Rother Valley Park?

Why are all the dead fish floating, on the water still and dark?

Why has everyone stopped boating, here in Rother Valley Park?

Mother, why is my skin burning? Each burn leaves behind a mark.

Why are all the leaves brown turning, here in Rother Valley Park?

Why is little Tommy staring, lying lifeless, still and stark?

All he did was breathe the air in, at the Rother Valley Park.

How soon will come the situation – a leaking tank, a careless spark?

Plant; village; school – just desolation – no more Rother Valley Park.

It was as I returned to my cold store on the Norwood Industrial Estate at about 10.00 am, as I turned the corner into

Ellisons Road, that I heard them. In the distance at the SARP UK gates were about 30 protesters. I drove down to where they were. Myra Turner, Brenda Glossop and Carol Dye were blocking the gates, holding up three tankers. Brian Ashmore stood with his wooden cross bearing the message "SARP OUT", looking out from under that black beret with his dark eyes as defiant as ever. Kevin Sampson was there too – he had taken to wearing a Freddy Kruger outfit, perhaps trying to challenge the Grim Reaper in the fashion stakes. Colin Williams was there with his daughter Samantha. Colin was a self-employed businessman; he sold tropical fish. Having a business that took him all over the country he spent many hours driving his large van, but whenever he had any spare time he was on the protests, as was Samantha.

"What are you all doing here? We hadn't arranged anything, had we?"

"No. A few of us got together last night and we all arranged to come down this morning," replied Margaret Ashmore.

"I think it is brilliant that you have done that amongst yourselves. Is there anything else that has happened?" I asked.

"We have got the EA inspectors out – the smells were terrible, we could hardly breathe. I don't know what they were up to, but the inspectors are on site now."

I returned to my van and, waving as I went, as I drove away I could see them in my rearview mirror: the tankers still there, the human barricade refusing to let them pass. At that moment the flashing blue lights of three police cars from the Derbyshire constabulary passed me. RASP had achieved its aims, disrupted the plant traffic, the operations. The EA were inspecting the site checking for leaks and keeping constant pressure on SARP UK. This morning had proved beyond doubt one thing – the protesters from RASP were so well-organised they could hold a protest and a blockade of the plant at an hour's notice without the help of Alistair. He had shown them how; now the pupils had become the masters.

Sunday arrived. Far from being the day off I once enjoyed, it was now taken up fully with arranging interviews with press, radio and TV for the following week, plus the weekly protest at the gates of SARP. That day I also had to sort out arrangements for my milk round while I was away on Friday and Saturday on the Paris protest. I arranged with my daughter Faye that she would cover my round while I was gone.

On Monday at about 7.00 am I was delivering on the Norwood Estate with my two helpers Chris Dutton and Sean Burgin when my mobile phone went. It was Radio Sheffield. They wanted to do an interview over the phone for their early-morning breakfast programme about the RASP/SARP campaign. The sight of me holding a radio interview with the BBC while also giving instructions like, "Two semi and a pasteurised to number 36, watch the dog," must have been strange.

The man doing the interview was a guy called Everard Davey. He started by saying the usual, "People are saying that you are all wasting your time at Killamarsh, that no campaign group in the UK has ever got rid of one of these incinerators and neither will RASP. What is your response to that?"

Letting my foot off the clutch to advance around Norwood Crescent, I clutched my mobile to my ear and replied, "My response to that is that we have no doubts we will win in the end. We will one day have this incinerator removed, we have this plant under 24-hour surveillance – any error, we will be the first to know. The EA are having to police the site for the first time."

"People are saying this is NIMBYism – not in my back yard. What is your response to that?"

"RASP's answer to that is that from the documents we were given by an ex-employee we know that Leigh Environmental were trying to find a new site, we have documents showing that the Killamarsh site was unfit and they wanted and applied for a transfer to Kirk Sandall near Doncaster in 1987. There was a huge protest by Doncaster residents and the plans were scrapped even though Leigh agreed to pay them £2 million for the site. It was people in Killamarsh that sent all our information to the protest group there and that was what stopped Leigh going. We wish it on no other community, we want the incinerator down and relocated far from residential areas."

He finished the interview with, "That was John Moran, Press Officer for the campaign group Residents Against SARP Pollution at Killamarsh."

That Monday we all packed the Crown for the meeting. Kevin Jones opened proceedings and covered the events of the previous week. "The meeting at the Village Centre was, as the paper headlines say, stunning. The revelations in the internal memos and files must have been a devastating blow to the company. Have you got any idea who left them, or are you not telling us, John?"

"I have no idea and that is the truth, but whoever had left them must have had a pretty responsible job somewhere in Leigh Environmental."

"Alistair, what are the arrangements for the trip to Paris this Thursday?"

"We are to meet at the Kwik Save car park at 8.30 pm, hopefully away for 9.00 pm in order to get on the early morning ferry from Dover. We still have four seats left if anyone knows anyone who may still want to go."

"I think we should invite four sixth-formers from Eckington School as observers; this is their village, a part of their history. We would not charge them anything, they should come as guests of RASP," was the response of David Parr.

"That seems a great idea. Who will go to Eckington School to speak with the headmaster?" asked Kevin.

"I will. I hope I have more success than with Mr. McLeavy," I replied.

The next morning, after finishing the round I returned home, washed and showered, and put on a suit and tie, as Sandra kept reminding me, "We don't all want to look scruffy all the time." There are times the flat cap and polo neck sweater have to come off, and this was one of those occasions.

Eckington School lies about three miles from Killamarsh as the crow flies, but you have to wind through Halfway and Mosborough to reach it. All the older children leaving the Sheffield Road schools go to Eckington, which was then a new school only about ten years old. The headmaster was now a Mr. Middlemass, but before him came Gerald Tracey, an ex-miner, a fact he repeated often with pride. Mr. Tracey, a man greatly respected by everyone, had been headmaster when my three children had gone to the school, from which Julian, my younger boy, had after RAF service gone on to study at St. John's College at Oxford.

I entered this modern school through the reception area, walked up to the desk and asked to speak to Mr. Middlemass.

"Is this concerning RASP, Mr. Moran?" The receptionist, who I had never met before, never asked my name. Our publicity had preceded both RASP and myself.

"It is RASP business," was my reply.

I was led into a modern headmaster's study. "John Moran, Press Officer, RASP." I held my hand out and Mr. Middlemass shook it and asked me to take a seat.

"What can I do for you?" he asked.

"I have come on behalf of Residents Against SARP Pollution. We are going to Paris on Thursday July 23 and we have four seats that we would like to offer four of your senior students, to act as observers. Since it is a part of Killamarsh history, we thought that they should be there to see it."

Mr. Middlemass walked around the table and said, "I thank RASP for their offer, but think that it would be inappropriate for them to come with you."

I did not argue. Whenever RASP asked Derbyshire County Council either directly or through their employees, the answer was always no. The reasons one day would become clear; at the moment we were dumbfounded.

Bev Smith had been appointed as Legal Officer at the formation of RASP. Bev knew as much about law as I knew about being a Press Officer – surprising how much you learn in such a short space of time. Bev had been organising a legal challenge to SARP UK. He and three other RASP members, Carol Dye, Margaret Marsh and June Cullabine, had enlisted the help of a specialist environmental law solicitor to oppose and close the plant by legal means. All four would be entitled to Legal Aid if a challenge was mounted as they were on low incomes. RASP had to pay for the initial solicitor request at about £200 in order to start proceedings; as our funds at the time were around £700 to £800 this did not present a problem. We at RASP saw it as another way to increase the already constant pressure that we were subjecting this company to.

The phone rang not long after I returned from Eckington School. "Steve Caddy here, John, can you tell me what this legal challenge to SARP is about?"

That night once again we had used the story to keep us in the public eye. Steve's report was headlined: "Controls Row at Toxic Scare Plant. Plant Not Being Policed, Says Lawyer." The main story read: "Environment watchdogs have been accused of failing to police a waste recycling plant responsible for two toxic scares. Solicitors addressing a public meeting in Killamarsh last night claimed the SARP UK plant was not being regulated properly by the

Environment Agency. Environmental law specialist Phil Shiner said he had found cause for concern after a preliminary study of public records. 'This waste plant should be subject to very, very tight control. Already I have major concerns about what I might find going through the public records documents,' he said. 'Last November the agency had told SARP to improve standards at its waste incinerator by fitting new equipment but the company had failed to do so. To my horror I found that SARP made an application at the end of March '98 to defer installation of the equipment. What we have here is a complete reversal of the legal position, which puts environmental concerns first, in favour of economic considerations. I have seen enough to make me think that this plant isn't being regulated properly by the Environment Agency and they know it.' If the Agency failed to act the lawyers would apply for a judicial review of their decision. But an agency spokeswoman denied it was failing in its duties. Mr. Shiner and his colleague Alastair Wallace have been called in by four residents to see what legal action can be taken to close the plant, currently being probed by the Agency and Health and Safety Executive."

It was just after midday on the next day, Tuesday, when the phone rang. I had managed about an hour's nap, about the maximum those days. The 3.00 starts, the milk round, trying to run my business, collecting all the weekly milk bills, every available minute talking to the media – it wasn't only SARP that was feeling the pressure. Along with all the people in RASP, we were being called on to find reserves, a lot had full-time jobs, there were mums with young children – it wasn't easy for any of us, but we had a common bond. The group always lifted you when you were feeling low; the thought of giving up was never a consideration.

I picked up the phone. It was ITV Yorkshire. "We want to do an interview with you. Can we meet outside the SARP gates?

"Yes, no problem," I replied.

I met the TV reporter about an hour later. We stood outside the SARP gate, close to the admin block that contained all the management and office staff, who were all up at the windows looking at the TV crew doing the interview. It clearly annoyed them as they sent this guy out who kept whistling constantly in an effort to disrupt the recording. I picked up on this and from then on I did all my press conferences outside the gates of SARP UK.

Chapter Seven

The Milkman Gets a Note from Le Président

The next day, as some wag in the press reported, "The milkman gets a note from the president." I had indeed received a note from Le Président on Vivendi-headed notepaper. It expressed concern at the issues raised and offered a visit to Vivendi's "superplant" at Limay, near Paris. Although Le Président himself would not be available to meet us, three of SARP's management team would be in Paris to discuss the situation in Killamarsh with the party from RASP – M. Philippe Martin, MD of SARP Industries, M. Philippe Girard, MD of SARP UK, and Martin Frobisher, site manager at Killamarsh.

At about 3.00 pm, the phone rang – it was Radio Hallam in Sheffield. I had faxed a copy of the letter to all the media.

"We want to do an interview over the phone, John."

"No problems," was my reply.

Within seconds I heard the news reporter introducing me on air. "We have John Moran, Press Officer from Residents Against SARP Pollution, or RASP, as they are known. What is your response to the President of Vivendi's letter, which asks to confirm you are all still going to Vivendi's headquarters in Paris and that they wish to confirm arrangements to visit their superplant at nearby Limay?"

"RASP has confirmed that we are coming to Paris to meet the two MDs of SARP Industries, M. Philippe Martin and M. Philippe Gerard. As regards the visit to the superplant at Limay, the answer to that is RASP is not interested in seeing any superplant. Our aim is getting rid of the clapped-out one in our own backyard."

"Thank you, John. Good luck to RASP in Paris." With that the phone went dead.

The next morning, Thursday July 23, I was up as usual at 3.00 am. I wanted to be finished in good time on the milk round as I had to make all the arrangements for the running of things, ordering my deliveries for the two mornings that I wouldn't be there. I managed to have a couple of hours' sleep; I knew that once we were on the coach we would not get any proper sleep till we got back on the Saturday. It was going to be a tough couple of days.

I arrived down at the Kwik Save car park at around 8.30 pm. The yellow and white Coopers' coach was standing there waiting to take us to Paris and the crowds were beginning to form to see us off. The light of that July evening was beginning to fade, but I could still make out the faces of all the villagers that were there. Though they were not active RASP members, they were supportive of us in all we did and lots were here tonight to show that. The Martin girls stood with their huge Residents Against SARP banner and there were placards everywhere: 'SARP MUST GO'; 'THE FUTURE'S NOT BRIGHT, THE FUTURE'S ORANGE – TAKE THE KILLER OUT OF KILLAMARSH'.

I took hold of the loudhailer and jumped up on the small wall at the corner of the car park. "I want to thank you all for coming to see us off tonight. It gives us great heart to see you all here, we will carry the voice of all our village to Paris. The owners of SARP UK will have to stop running; there will be no place left for them to go when we stand outside the doors of No. 52 Rue d'Anjou. We will not let you down, we will make sure they hear us, they will know we have been."

I could see the RASP members one by one climbing the steps of the Coopers' coach. David and Margaret Parr, followed by Margaret and Brian Ashmore, Carol Dye just about to get on, given a last-minute kiss by her daughter Beverley whilst husband Terry looked on, Pat Whitehouse our secretary, Brenda Glossop, Myra Turner and Tony Ward.

They were all taking up seats whilst family members stood on the pavements talking up to those already sitting near the windows. The Martin girls had folded their banner and were putting it into the huge luggage compartment on the coach to add to all the RASP banners and placards that we would need on the march through Paris. Alistair, in his familiar dark jacket, was helping them with Becky Fryer. There were two TV crews travelling with us – BBC Look North and Yorkshire ITV Calendar News, as well as reporters from *The Sheffield Star*.

I climbed the stairs. I was just about the last to board, the coach was packed as I made my way down to where Sandra was sitting towards the back. Three seats in front of me sat the figure of Alan Charles and his daughter, the sole representative of all of the Derbyshire County, District and Parish Councils, who was here as much as a member of RASP as an elected member of the Derbyshire County Council. RASP was, as usual, fighting this front on its own.

The coach moved slowly forward and edged out on to the Sheffield Road, turning right to pass the Village Centre and then starting to climb Lock Hill. The crowds were all along the roads on either side as we passed the Sheffield Road schools, clapping – hundreds had turned out that night. We made our way up the hill that led to Barlborough and the M1. I turned to look back. I could see all of the village below and to the right on the edge of the Rother Valley was SARP UK, its site lights like a ship in the almost faded light with the outline of the huge incinerator against the night sky.

The Ml was only three miles from the village and we had soon joined it to head south for Dover. There was lots of talking and laughter for the first hour or so, with much to discuss as to what awaited us in Paris. Then the noise started to die down, people starting to make the most of their temporary sleeping accommodation. The driver dimmed the lights.

Sandra turned to me and said, "Are you going to read that story, that story Owd Tup gave you?"

Dave Froggatt had pushed some of his prolific writings into my hand as we were getting on the coach. "Everybody likes a fairy story" was all he said as he passed me the papers with a twinkle in his eyes. I made my way down to the front of the coach where the drivers were sitting, the only light coming from the small aisle lights at either side.

I took the driver's microphone and asked, "Would anyone like a bedtime story, a fairy story?"

"Oh yes." I think it was mostly the female voices that answered, childhood memories just for a short while remembered.

"Then I will begin…

"Fairy Apathy, or When the Clouds Roll By

"Once upon a time – that's how all good fairy tales begin – once upon a time there was a tiny little village called Happymarsh. It was called Happymarsh because all the people who lived there were happy, friendly people, all the children played happily together and always did what their mums and dads told them. The sun shone every day and it only rained for two hours each night. The people did not even know what a cloud looked like. Even the pig farm smelled sweet.

"This was not really a fairy story at the beginning, because at first there were no fairies in Happymarsh; you see, the people were so kind and good and happy that there was no need for good fairies, and it was not big or important enough for witches and bad fairies to practise their spells and wicked ways.

"But then the land was taken over by a far-off king called EEC. And the first thing that King EEC and his courtiers did was to make the people of Happymarsh forsake their money, weights, measures and many of their old customs and use EEC money, weights, measures and customs instead. And then one day, someone at the palace of EEC discovered that there were no fairies in Happymarsh and told the king, who decreed that henceforth, all places must have at least one good and one bad fairy. But the people of Happymarsh were not allowed to choose their own fairies, and had to have ones chosen from afar.

"The Good Fairy was young and pretty, and not very experienced at magic. When she came to Happymarsh, she found there was little for her to do as the people were all so good and kind, and so she sat around all day, eating chocolates, reading magazines and watching telly. After a while, even when the simplest bit of magic was needed, she couldn't be bothered, and so it was easy for her archenemy, the Bad Fairy, to quietly go about her evil ways.

"The Bad Fairy was old, ugly and crotchety, and spent all her time working out new and more powerful wicked spells. When she saw that she had little or no opposition from the Good Fairy, she sent for her old friend, Baron Hugh. K. Sarp. Baron Sarp brought with him a band of sorcerers and alchemists who could turn rubbish into gold, and they set up huge cauldrons and simmered in these all kinds of things which they gathered from far and near. They worked all day and night; their fires were always burning and giving off strange smoke and smells. And the people of Happymarsh were suddenly not so happy and they changed the name of the village to Notsohappymarsh. And then when the pig farm began to smell to rival Sarp's smells, when the people grew irritable because they had to close their doors and windows and when the children too were affected and began to squabble among themselves, they changed its name again to Worrymarsh.

"That was when they asked the Good Fairy, Fairy Apathy, to help them and earn her stipend. But as there had been nothing good for her to do for so long, she had grown fat and lazy, her wand was all rusty, and she couldn't even turn frogs back into princes, so the people told her she must pull herself together or they would stop her chocolate. One day, there was a big bang, the sky went dark and a huge orange cloud floated over the village. The people rushed out, saw the menacing cloud and were afraid, for don't forget, they had never seen a cloud before, much less a dark orange one. 'What manner of thing is this?' they wondered and rushed into their houses, closing their doors and windows tight. And when they asked Baron Sarp what this strange thing called a toxic cloud was, he told them not to worry, for it would only harm them if it touched them, or got into their eyes, or they breathed it in. But the people did not really believe him, especially when he told them that it could not happen again.

"And so, when a few days later yet another orange cloud darkened the skies, the people were really frightened. And the village was then called Fearmarsh. They gathered together to see how they could rid themselves of the evil Baron Sarp and his minions. They advertised for a pied piper, but the musicians' union informed them that pied pipers could only be employed to rid towns of rats of the four-legged variety. They sought to revoke the Baron's licence, but were told the tablets were written in stone. They marched with banners to where the Baron made his smells. They sent a message to King EEC and all his underlings, telling of their fears for their children, who were living under a cloud.

"Meanwhile, Fairy Apathy was ashamed for not protecting them, so she went to Weightwatchers and became once more slim and pretty, she cleaned up her rusty wand with Duraglit, and went to the village library to read up on anti-Sarp spells. Having done all this, she stood on tiptoe, waved her shiny magic wand and chanted her magic spell. 'Away with the bad fairy's spells, away with all the noxious smells! Away with toxic clouds I say, away with Sarp, away, away! Away!'

"Now, whether it was the meeting, or the march, or the message to EEC, whether at last Fairy Apathy had got her act together, or whether Baron Sarp had made enough gold and decided to move to pastures new, we will never know, but suddenly, there was a big flash and when the dust had settled, gone was Baron Sarp, gone were his sorcerers and alchemists, and the Bad Fairy knew she had met her match and had to be content with only performing nasty little bits of magic like making the buses leave early, traffic lights stay on red and letting everyone know what was going to happen in the next episode of their favourite soap. When Sarp and his minions had vanished, everyone was happy once more so they once again changed the name of the village – yes you've guessed it, back to Happymarsh. Then they all lived (more or less) happy ever after.

"Mind you, the pig farm still smells now and it rains most days, and the children are occasionally heard to squabble, and even, now and then, not do as their mummy tells them, but then even in fairy stories you can't have everything. Oh yes, and the man who was on a nice little earner making new village signs became redundant and turned to painting landscapes for a living. He doesn't sell many though; for some reason he always paints the clouds.

"GOVERNMENT HEALTH WARNING: Children should not play with toxic clouds even if a stranger says they are quite safe, and remember – not all fairy tales have a happy ending."

I had been accompanied all the way through as if it was a pantomine – Baron Hugh K. Sarp had been booed at every opportunity and the applause for Owd Tup's writing was long and loud. As I made my way back up the dimly lit aisle of the coach, I thought a bit of laughter was no bad thing, a little relief from the long journey and difficult task that lay ahead.

The whole coach then settled down to a couple of hours' snatched sleep. I woke as the coach entered the outskirts of Dover. The streets were virtually deserted, with only the odd car and container lorry heading for the port. We arrived on the quayside and waited our turn to go up the rear ramp of the P&O Stena Line passenger ferry. The bright lights of the ferry contrasted with the darkness of the water and the surrounding large car parking area. We slowly went up the ramp onto the ferry, where we made our way up to the top deck. We all stood on the deck as the ferry slid out of the port.

Vivendi, Générale des Eaux, or SARP UK – whatever you are called, we are on our way.

Chapter Eight

On the Champs-Élysées

We left Calais behind and were soon passing open countryside. It was a beautiful July morning, not a cloud in the sky. We stopped at a motorway cafe about an hour or so from Paris, where we were met by a continental breakfast. It was not to everyone's taste but the morning coffee was welcome and woke us all up. We were all ready for our protest on the streets of Paris.

We entered the outskirts of Paris and headed to what seemed to be the very middle of the city. It was then that Steve Martin's mobile rang. It was Julian Worricker from BBC Five Live in London, asking to speak to John Moran, Press Officer for RASP. I heard him telling the nation, "There is a coach full of protesters driving towards the centre of Paris. They are from the small village of Killamarsh in North

East Derbyshire, who are trying to close down a waste recycling plant and its toxic burning incinerator. We are now going to speak to John Moran, the Press Officer for Residents Against SARP Pollution, or RASP, as they are known. John, can you tell us why you are in Paris, what you are going to do today and what the group's aims are?"

"We are here in Paris today because this company, SARP UK, and its predecessor Leigh Environmental have poisoned and polluted our small village for the last 20 years. The health of our children and all the residents is suffering. We repeatedly asked the company to meet us and they have refused to do so. We come to Paris today to end the running away, today they have run out of places to go, we are going to their headquarters in Paris. The answer to the second question is that we want this incinerator out of our village and this waste plant moved away from us."

"Thank you, John. That was the environmental protest group RASP on their…" We never heard him finish the sentence, we had driven into one of the many underpasses near to the centre of Paris and the mobile phone connection had been lost.

The coach came up the Champ d'Élysées to let the camera crews off. We continued around what must qualify as one of the biggest roundabouts in Europe, the Arc de Triomphe, before heading down the beautiful wide tree-lined roads to the Place Saint-Augustin, where the coach came to a halt. The driver asked us to be back at 7.30 pm that evening in order to catch the ferry from Calais that night. The time was just after 9.00 am when the first of the group piled off the coach and headed for the luggage area at the side to unload all the banners and placards. What all the Paris office workers made of the mini invasion of "beaucoup d'Anglais" is anybody's guess, but the look of curiosity on the faces of the very chic ladies and equally smart gentlemen was something that would live long in the memory.

We had all assembled, led by the Martin sisters and their huge banner, Carol Dye wearing a little black trilby and a red short-sleeved jumper with the loudhailer on a strap around her shoulder. Cradling the megaphone with her left hand and holding the mike with the other, she looked more French than the French. Following behind were Alistair, Becky, Alan Charles and his daughter, Tony Ward, David and Margaret Parr, Ann and Trevor Cockerill, then Steve Martin – about 50 in all.

We started to turn onto the Boulevard Malershebes; there on the corner waiting for us was the Grim Reaper. We marched down to the Rue d'Anjou, passersby amazed by the black-costumed Reaper, scythe in hand, followed by Carol Dye giving a very good shot at the French language explaining why we were there. The loudhailer was certainly working overtime. We also handed out leaflets written in

French explaining why we were on the streets of Paris that July morning.

We arrived at 52 Rue d'Anjou. We had left the wide tree-lined avenues – this road was much smaller, with those lovely cream-coloured buildings that seemed to be everywhere in Paris. Number 52 Rue d'Anjou was the original home of Vivendi under the name of Générale des Eaux. From its formation in 1853 it had mainly been the water company of France, but since the 1980s it had diversified into waste management and railways. The entrance was more like a stable block, with gates that led into a kind of courtyard. Our arrival had not been unexpected; armed security guards blocked our way.

Alistair was the first to confront them.

"We have come from Killamarsh in England to speak with the MDs of SARP Industries and the head of SARP UK." He made Killamarsh seem like the centre of the universe; I suppose to us it seemed as if it was.

The guards made no reply, nor did they attempt to get a second opinion from the absent MDs. It was then that I took the loudhailer and announced to the whole of the Rue D'Anjou that we had come on an almost 2,000-mile roundtrip from North East Derbyshire and we would not let any traffic in or out of these gates until we had met M. Martin, M. Girard and Martin Frobisher, the Killamarsh site manager.

TWO CLOUDS TOO MANY   137

RASP in the City of Light… Our campaigning activity saw a group of ordinary people end up in some unexpected places, in this case bringing our message to the Paris streets when we paid a visit to Vivendi, SARP UK's parent company. Above are shown Tony Ward (holding placard), Julie Martin standing next to the famous banner, Carol Dye, Trevor Cockerill (wearing sunglasses) and Alan Charles on the loudhailer.

The sound of "SARP UK, hear us say, take your toxic waste away! What do we want? Close down SARP UK! When do we want it? We want it now!" rang out around the Paris streets. Within ten minutes, the whole of the Rue D'Anjou was blocked and people were hanging out of office windows to see what all the commotion was about. It might have been ignored by Vivendi outside those old green gates at the bottom of Ellisons Road, but in the heart of Paris it was another story.

Very soon a tall English guy came out of the door on the left-hand side of the arch. We knew him as working for the PR company that SARP had employed after the leaks in May – they were costing SARP in excess of £10,000 a week and up to now they were proving a complete disaster.

"We want to speak to the three men, where are they?" Alistair shouted. Voices were raised, the guards looked menacing, but we had not come all this way to stand in the street.

"We will allow four people in to meet with the directors," the Englishman announced. He was as good at reading the situation as he was at PR – four people walked in after him and another 30 followed. The next thing I knew we were in a huge boardroom with a long, highly polished table. At the top was a chair that could only have been for the President, Jean-Marie Messier. My everlasting memory of the Générale des Eaux boardroom was the sight of an 11-year-old boy in a Sheffield Wednesday shirt sitting in the President's chair, from which on other days the fate of 325,000 employees would be decided.

From a little room adjoining came what I thought were three very nervous and frightened-looking men. The PR man introduced us to M. Philippe Martin, M. Philippe Girard and

Martin Frobisher, the latter of whom we were well acquainted with being the site manager at Killamarsh.

I was the first to speak. "I have here all the evidence you should have had before you took this site over last year. The state of the tanks, 60 to 70 years old, that have never been metal-tested, the same as the one that split apart on May 30." I continued, "Page after page of complaints from the people of Killamarsh to the Environment Agency about the smells and fumes from this site caused by your incinerator, the same incinerator that Leigh Environmental bought from Berridge at Hucknall near Mansfield. The same incinerator that was refused planning permission because it was unsafe. It was allowed to be installed on the Killamarsh site, a collusion between Leigh and the Environment Agency at Rotherham."

David Parr then took over. "We have come here today to tell you that we have 60 percent asthma in our schools, children cannot play out without the daily fears of toxic clouds from your decaying plant. Babies being born with defects far in excess of what we would expect in a village our size."

Ann Cockerill was the next that the beleaguered trio had to contend with. "They are not your children and grandchildren that are being poisoned day after day; if they were, how long would you keep the plant open then?"

Philippe Martin held his hands up. "We do regret the incidents at Killamarsh, they were the result of a pre-existing problem. The safety record is not up to the standard of our other plants."

"No, no, we don't trust you no more than we trusted Leighs – all the staff at the site are ex-Leigh men, management, office staff and drivers." Steve Martin was making sure he had his say. The debate went on for what seemed a long time, in fact close on an hour and a half. We had our say, we had come well informed, with documents, files and information that SARP were never given or they had not asked for prior to the takeover of Leigh Environmental.

Alistair stepped forward as the meeting was about to close and at his signal I walked forward to his side. He then said to our French hosts, "We have a petition signed by 7,000 people in Killamarsh for the closure of your plant. Our MP Harry Barnes has today delivered this petition on our behalf to the Houses of Parliament in London and at our request has asked the Environment Minister Mr. Michael Meacher to come to Killamarsh to see for himself the daily problems we face with your plant."

M. Philippe Girard then made his only contribution. "We are going to stick to our plans for improving the facility until it meets the SARP Industries standards in France and around the world. I am ready to go to Killamarsh but there is no chance of the incinerator and plant closing down."

With shouts from RASP of, "We will see about that," and "That's what you think," we were on our way out, leaving the three men as quickly as we had come. We had delivered the message. We would now deliver the rest to No. 42 Avenue de Friedland, the offices of Vivendi just off the Champs-Élysées across the road from the Arc de Triomphe. Heading along the Rue d'Anjou, we turned left on to the Rue La Boétie and right on to the Champs-Élysées. The streets were now full of office workers and shoppers. The Grim Reaper led us, followed by Carol Dye and myself just in front of the Martin girls. As we marched we handed our leaflets out to whoever would take them. The crowds on the wide pavements parted and we were applauded all the way by the Parisians. There was nothing, it would seem, the French liked more than a protest; they always have plenty of their own. Carol Dye, loudhailer in hand, was speaking what sounded to me like fluent French to the parted crowds. Finally we arrived at the offices of Vivendi. There was no way we were going to be allowed in, guards stood across the doors. We assembled around them – if we weren't going in then neither was anyone else, and nor was anyone coming out. The Grim Reaper stood in front of the guards. Alistair was now on the loudhailer, David Parr to his left with a placard reading, "VIVENDI SAUVER VIE FERMER SARP". I didn't speak much French but I got the message, as did the hundreds of people who had gathered to see what it was all about.

The appearance of the two TV crews did nothing to dampen down the interest in our protest. Notebook in hand,

Mike Ellis, the press man from one of our local papers who had travelled with us, asked as the television cameras moved closer, "John, what has your protest group RASP done today that you could not do in Killamarsh?"

"We have come here today because for the last two months we have asked for Vivendi, owners of SARP UK, to speak with us – we have today forced them to listen. We have brought this petition signed by 7,000 people – we 50 are the voice of those thousands and today they were heard here on the streets of Paris."

With that one of the TV presenters turned to camera and said, "From the heart of Paris and the protest group RASP I return you to the studios of Yorkshire Television in Leeds."

We had noticed all the time our protest had been going on the presence of about six riot vans containing the French Special Police, the ones with the strange small hats. They were watching us, several standing outside their vehicles; they were waiting to see if our protest would become violent, but that was not the way of our group. At around midday our protest had lasted almost three hours and we decided to call it a day. We had done everything we had set out to do, it had been a most embarrassing day for one of France's premier companies. We agreed to meet up later in order to be on the coach for just after 7.00 pm.

Sandra and I headed for a restaurant quite close by. "What a state we are in," were her first words as we found a table. The place was packed. We did look awful. Sandra had been up at 5.00 am on Thursday and had come directly to the coach from work in order to be with us. We had had no chance to shower. Yes, as I said, we looked and felt terrible and we were only halfway through this trip. We finished our meal, then walked to a park where, finding a grassy area, I simply lay down and crashed out. I awoke later having been asleep for three or four hours; I would feel better for that, I knew, but it had done nothing for my appearance. We made our way back to the Place Saint-Augustin, where the welcome sight of our coach was waiting for us. The yellow and white coach bearing the words Coopers of Killamarsh weaved its way through the fading Paris light. We were on our way home.

The coach pulled into the Kwik Save car park at just after six on the Saturday morning. The only welcoming committee was one man on a little street-cleaning vehicle, who briefly glanced over then continued on his way. We arrived back home at around 6.15. I had a shower followed by breakfast; I had to be at the Community Inquiry being held at the St. Giles Church Hall in the village for 11.00 am.

When we arrived at the church hall, as usual the place was packed. Ken Coates MEP was on the panel, which also included Dr. William R. Gray of Eckington, Dr. Jon Dale of Bolsover and Hugh Ellis of the Coalfield Planning Co-op.

The meeting was opened by Ken Coates, who asked members of the audience to relate their experiences living in Killamarsh and any health problems they or their families were having. The doctors, when questioned, painted a very different picture to one given by the Derbyshire Health Chief Medical Officer who had spoken at a recent public meeting I had attended, at which she said relatively speaking we had no more problems than people living in the Peak District around Matlock. The dangers of living near a waste incinerator were explained fully by Dr. Jon Dale, who told the meeting, "A friend of mine, one of the leading medical figures in the UK on pollution, Dick van Steenis, has publicly said that toxic waste dumps are extremely dangerous, he has said that in Wales they have two – one in the Rhondda, one near Merthyr Tydfil. The infant mortality rate around both of them had risen to the levels of Belarus after Chernobyl. The local councils set them up as waste sites and then the Environment Agency converted them to toxics; once a council passes a site the Environment Agency has powers to impose toxic wastes there, with no appeal and no public consultation. He noticed that certain areas were being absolutely clobbered by pollution with high concentrations of polluting industrial sites. You'll find that the areas with the worst mortality rates in this country are also in the areas with the worst pollution from industry. The regulatory system is hopeless, because the EA gets money from importing the toxic waste, from authorising it and policing it. They are supposed to be the ones prosecuting but they don't, because they would jeopardise their own finances by shutting it down; 60 percent of their income comes from their fees from industry. It's like having the police being financed by the drug barons."

Without doubt we at RASP were well aware of the 'cosy' relationship between Leigh and latterly SARP UK with the Environment Agency. Now everything was starting to become much clearer.

The meeting ended about 2.00 pm. As we were leaving, Ken Coates MEP crossed the hall. He held out his hand. "Congratulation to all you RASP members, we all followed your visit to Paris, your group were on every local TV news report and radio, as well as all the main newspapers in the area all weekend. We thought you all were so brave to protest down the streets of Paris, especially with all those riot police standing so near. I don't think there has ever been a protest group go to Paris before, not that we can remember."

That was RASP. Always original, different, that was why we believed we would win this campaign against SARP UK in the end. I went home after the meeting; Sandra had already gone to bed. She had not had any sleep for nearly three days, 62 hours she later informed me. I was out on my feet. It had been a hard three days. I went to bed and never woke till 10.00 am on the Sunday.

Kevin Jones opened the Monday meeting at the Crown. "What an unbelievable week we have had. A very well done to all those who went to Paris, you were all quite brilliant, from seeing the Coopers' coach go round the Arc de Triomphe, to Carol Dye and the Grim Reaper marching through the centre of Paris leading you. Fantastic."

The resulting applause was deafening from the 200 or so who packed the building that night. "Well, I will hand over to Alistair, I know we have a lot of things to get through."

"We certainly have. We seem to be having protests, incidents if not on a daily basis, then at least two or three times a week. We find ourselves in the media spotlight almost all of the time, we are really hurting this company. We have to keep going, there is no middle ground. As someone said once before, it's them or us. This week, on Thursday, it has been confirmed that Michael Meacher, the Minister for the Environment for the Labour government, is to visit Killamarsh and, in his words, 'I was asked by Mr. Harry Barnes MP when presenting a 7,000-signed petition from the community organised by RASP, if I would come to Killamarsh and see the problems the community are having. I also want to visit the SARP UK site before I decide on anything.'"

"Well, that is the first time in Killamarsh's long history that a Minister of the Crown has visited our village, so that's a first," Wendy Wellings added.

"We need to organise a protest for Thursday teatime. He is due to get to the plant at about 4.30 pm, accompanied by

Harry Barnes. He will be shown the site by Philippe Martin and Philippe Girard, and site manager Martin Frobisher. I suggest we alert everyone by the telephone tree, speak to everyone – we want as many as we can get there. After the site visit he is going down to the Village Centre where he will have a meeting with County, District and Parish Councillors, and also he wants to meet four members of RASP."

"Wow, a government official has actually said they wanted to meet RASP, that's another first," added Ian Legge. Ian had only recently joined the group, he had experience in chemicals having been employed in the industry. Now self-employed, his expertise would help us in the coming months.

"Who are the four people that we should put forward?" was Alistair's next question.

"Roger Barraclough, definitely," said Brian Ashmore.

"I think that David Parr should, he has been on both campaign groups, in 1986 and then now," Myra Turner added.

"Ann Nettleship," I always admired the way Ann spoke in public, I had no hesitation in putting her forward.

"Just one more then," Alistair said. "I think our Press Officer should be there, just in case another story pops up, it usually manages to." I was to be the fourth representative of RASP. "I want you all to speak to Mr. Meacher about how this plant affects you and your family personally. You, Roger, as a businessman; you, Ann, as a mum; David, you as someone who has been involved in two campaigns over the last 12 years and how it affects you; and, John, I want you to talk about the internal memos and the state of the site. When the protest is finished and Mr. Meacher leaves the site, we will all go down to the Village Centre, they are going to have loudspeakers all around the car park so we will be able to listen to what is going on inside the meeting."

The meeting was just ending when someone's mobile rang; it was Tracey Nettleship's. Her mother Ann had called to say that the Toxic Night Shift had been forced to run for the safety of their cars to get out of the way of horrendous toxic smells coming from the plant, that they were down there now and were waiting for the EA to arrive.

"I think this calls for the cavalry." Kevin Sampson was keen to join his wife Allison, one of the mainstays of the Toxic Night Shift.

"Are we going to join them?" Alistair's words were lost in the sound of chairs being pushed back and the ensuing rush to cars that would take us to the gates of SARP.

The toxic smells that greeted us as we opened our car doors were unbelievable. Whatever they had been up to on site had gone, as usual, disastrously wrong, but now there was no hiding place for their mistakes. The darkness and lies, the non-attendance of the EA until the next day, thanks to the Toxic Night Shift, were a thing of the past. Ann, her sister June Cullabine and Allison met us.

"The EA are in there now, they have been in about an hour. They came out within 30 minutes of our phone call, they had handkerchiefs over their faces, they will not be able to use the old excuse, 'No noticeable smell, will revisit site if necessary.'"

The difference in visiting the site at the time of the call rather than 18 hours later was obvious. Two hours later the EA emerged; by that time we had about five toxic tankers backing up Ellisons Road and another three trying to get out. The two hours had not been wasted. BBC Radio Sheffield had been alerted, and they had been joined by the rest of the media – another SARP disaster would be reported tomorrow morning.

The editorial in the following evening's *Sheffield Star* said, "SARP UK has become a byword for error. Last night, local residents had to flee toxic fumes and smells at the SARP UK plant. Protesters holding their nightly protest were driven back by the toxic fumes. In a statement by the Environment Agency they said, 'The staff at SARP UK were transferring toxic sludge from a tank to the landfill site when residues were left on the ground producing an odour that could be detected beyond the perimeters of the site.'"

The next morning we intercepted a letter from the EA to SARP from Colin Guest, the officer based at Rotherham, and released it to the media. It was in all the press within 24 hours. It read, "Leaving these residues in this state would, under any circumstances, be wholly unacceptable. It is even more unbelievable that with the current level of scrutiny upon your facility, that such unacceptable practises should occur."

SARP's response was, "They are just housekeeping problems"; however, the EA felt it necessary to deliver an official warning to SARP to change its cleaning process after this latest leak. A plant manager was disciplined for leaving toxic sludge lying round the plant.

The next day, Wednesday July 29, the day before the visit of Michael Meacher, I was putting a speech together to present to him at the Leisure Centre, along with the other three RASP members who had been nominated to speak to him. I finished the speech later that evening and decided that as I had another long day tomorrow I would have an early night. The next morning I finished the milk round and did my weekly accounts for the milk. I intended to be down at SARP for about 4.15 pm in order to join the protest.

Chapter Nine

Minister, Did They Show You the Rocket Fuel?

It was about 1.00 that afternoon. I was in my study when a knock came at the door, more than likely a milk customer with holiday dates who forgot to leave me a note, the usual scenario. Then I heard Sandra say, "Please come in, John will be with you in a minute."

I rose from my chair and as I passed Sandra, she said, "There's someone to see you, he's waiting in the front room."

The man waiting was in his forties with receding black hair; I thought I knew him vaguely. "I must talk with you, John, about SARP, there is something that Michael Meacher should know, and I want you and RASP to tell him for me. I'm on a short-term contract working for SARP UK. I have written down everything you need to tell him." And with that from his inside pocket he withdrew an envelope.

"Read it when I am gone," was the only thing he said before he stood up and moved to go.

I showed him out and thanked him, and as he was about to close the gate behind him, I asked, "What made you come?"

"My kids, like the rest of us."

I never saw or spoke to the man again.

That afternoon, I made my way down to SARP. I went a different way, down Sheffield Road to the top of Lock Hill to where the road crosses the now disused Chesterfield to Worksop canal. I turned right along the old towpath that runs at the back of Primrose Lane. Passing the last cottage, I looked across and wondered if our poet Owd Tup was busy penning another poem to add to the ever increasing number he had already written about the RASP battle with SARP UK.

Following the towpath, the view opened up – I could now see Killamarsh below to my left and in front the Rother Valley Country Park. A few hundred yards along the towpath, there was SARP UK. I was approaching the plant from the rear. The old green storage tanks had been repainted by the company to give the place a facelift, but it was a tired and decaying place, no amount of fresh green paint would ever change that. There, about 50 yards from where I was standing, was what will always symbolise SARP UK and what all we hated about this place. Rising high into the sky, the sun glinting off its surface in the bright afternoon, was the incinerator. The last part of my approach to the site was on the road past Alan Cooper's, where the coach stood that had taken us to Paris. The time was about 4.15.

From where I was I could already hear them: hundreds of protesters at the gates of SARP. Ellisons Road was already blocked by the crowds, including lots of mothers with their children. The Derbyshire Education Committee couldn't stop or threaten them now that the school day was over. The banners and placards were everywhere: 'MICHAEL MEACHER STICK TO ELECTION PLEDGES', 'RASP', 'NEVER AGAIN, CLOSE DOWN SARP, SUMMER IN KILLAMARSH', a placard showing two faces wearing gas masks. 'MR. MEACHER GIVE US FRESH AIR TO BREATHE.' The message was everywhere.

Michael Meacher, the Minister for the Environment in Tony Blair's Labour government, would soon see for himself. There were two police standing on either side of the first green and white SARP toxic tanker. The driver sat resigned to the fact that this was not his lucky day – as the crowds kept reminding him, "You and your toxic load are going nowhere."

Then the blue flashing lights of two police cars announced the arrival of Michael Meacher. He walked from his car flanked on his left by our MP Harry Barnes, walking with the aid of a stick after his recent heart attack, and on his right by a police sergeant with his hands on the lapels of the yellow police top that covered his dark uniform. Michael Meacher came towards the crowds, a tall, handsome man, greying at the temples, bespectacled and dark-suited with a blue and white spotted tie. I looked at him closely and I liked him; there was something about him. I knew he was an environmentalist, I felt he would listen, we would get a fair hearing.

He stopped to face the crowd with his back to the first tanker. Taking the loudhailer from Carol Dye, he addressed the throng. "I am extremely disturbed by the two toxic leaks that have happened at this site, I can understand your concerns here, so I have come to see for myself. I have been offered a tour of the site and I am going to do that now. I would ask you if you would allow the road to be cleared whilst I go on site."

With that the crowds parted and the previously resigned driver of the first tanker and the rest of his colleagues got a lucky break. The protesters watched as Meacher, accompanied by Philippe Martin, Philippe Girard and Martin Frobisher, all wearing regulation hard hats and yellow reflective jackets, crossed the site. We followed round the outer perimeter fence to see where they took him. We could see him near to the incinerator and moving on, past all the drums of chemicals that were stored on site. We were told that there were as many as 15,000 drums, and the EA had told them to reduce them to under 5,000.

An hour and a half later, Michael Meacher appeared in the doorway of SARP's block. The two Frenchmen and Martin Frobisher at his side, he walked slowly to his car. The car moved slowly through the SARP gates, increasing its speed as the lines of police formed a passage through the crowds of protesters. The protesters now all followed, most on foot, they were all making for the Village Centre, keen to know what the Minister of the Environment intended to do about our neighbour on the edge of the Rother Valley.

I made my way down Sheffield Road. The streets were full of people – the visit of someone as important as Michael Meacher had raised the stakes in our campaign, and people who had sat on the fence since the two incidents in May and in truth for many years past were now involved.

The meeting was to be held in the main hall of the Village Centre, there were council officials and police on the doors; they had a list and only those on the list were being allowed in. The whole meeting was being relayed over loudspeakers to the crowds outside, who were standing with their banners and placards, whilst Alistair and Carol Dye took turns on the loudhailer. The doors to the meeting were closed. I sat at the rear about five rows back; in front of me I could see in the middle of the front row Harry Barnes, MP for

Dronfield and the Gosforth Valley, Alan Charles, Derbyshire County Councillor, John Holden, Jayne Holden and Bob Harper and Grant Laughton, at only 22, Chairman of our Parish Council. On the second row sat representatives of the local emergency services, fire, ambulance and police, and Chris Roslyn-Josephs, a Sheffield councillor who represented the Beighton/Mosborough area. Seated in front of me were Roger Barraclough, Ann Nettleship and David Parr; I sat on my own.

The meeting was opened by Grant Laughton, who thanked Michael Meacher. The Minister sat on his own facing the meeting at a slightly raised table at the front. "I would like to thank the Minister for coming to Killamarsh today. That you come at a time of great concern and unease in our village is unfortunate, but it is a visit welcomed by the Killamarsh Parish Council and the residents."

The leader of the Parish Council then said, "I would like to introduce to you, Minister, people I feel can explain the effect that SARP UK has on the village."

John Holden was the first to speak. He gave a brief history of the village and how the community had worked hard to overcome the economic decline of the 1980s: the effect of the miners' strike and pit closures, the high unemployment and the savage government cuts in Council spending affecting all aspects of public services. "The community has also suffered from other major environmental problems. Open-casting ripped out the 'marsh' from Killamarsh and and left us with noise, dust and a lunar landscape." John then went on to tell everyone what the Parish Council had done over the last ten years: sports centres, training centres… I could not believe, however admirable the achievements had been, that they were being aired here, when the purpose, or at least RASP's purpose, was to close this waste plant, remove the incinerator and shut down SARP UK.

The next person to speak was Alan Charles, who at least got down to the nitty-gritty. "People think that Killamarsh is a dangerous place – they don't want to move here, new businesses are reluctant to set up near to a source of pollution and people are concerned about the value of their homes. In all, there are worries and uncertainties about our future. SARP argue their economic case for not moving. We say, 'We cannot afford for you to stay – either economically, socially or, most importantly, in terms of our community health." Well, that's more like it, were my first thoughts. Alan Charles had been the only one of our elected officials that had spoken RASP's language.

Chris Roslyn-Josephs was the next to speak. "I represent 20,000 people in the areas bordering the Rother Valley Country Park and we fully support the RASP campaign. Pollution problems do not stop at borders and everyone is affected by the noise and odours from the SARP plant."

Grant Laughton then said he would introduce some residents of the village to speak, as always carefully wording his introduction so that the name RASP was not mentioned, a stance that would be taken for the rest of the campaign and long into the distant future. "Mr. David Parr."

"I want to talk about the everyday problems suffered by villagers. Problems of smells, noise, pollution and the fear of accidents from the site are suffered 24 hours a day, 365 days a year. Particular problems have been experienced with the sewers, and the smells have seeped into cellars of houses on the Sheffield Road. We feel that this has to end and we look to you, Mr. Meacher, to help us sort out these problems."

David sat down and Roger Barraclough stood up.

"My name is Roger Barraclough, I am a local businessman in the village. More importantly, I am a father of two young children who attend the Sheffield Road school. My deepest concern is the closeness of this site to these schools, the daily fear of the next big explosion, the one that these schools with our children in don't survive. We all know it is not 'if' but 'when'. The clock is ticking, if we don't do something it will be too late."

Ann Nettleship rose to her feet. After introducing herself she continued, "I campaigned against Leigh in 1986.

With many more parents in this village we have had to live with the fears of explosions and dioxins from this plant. In 1986, everyone told us not too worry, yet 12 years later two huge toxic clouds were released, the village cut off twice from the outside world in the space of 14 days, our children are suffering, there are high levels of asthma, young mothers suffering miscarriages, babies being born with birth defects. We know from RASP – that is Residents Against SARP Pollution, Minister—" she turned to Michael Meacher "—we know at RASP that living close to a toxic waste plant is the reason why we are suffering such high problems, and I ask not only for myself as a mother, not only for RASP, but for all of our residents and for the future generations to come to close this plant and end the suffering." As Ann sat down I saw the look in Michael Meacher's eye. That was one devastating speech, I could see she had got to him... Ann, what a wasted talent you are, I thought, how glad I am that you are with RASP tonight.

I was the only one left to speak. Grant Laughton looked towards me and I rose slowly to my feet. How a few months in this campaign had changed me, no longer sitting in the hope that no one asked me to say anything, sitting in dread at being asked to speak in front of meetings and crowds. I looked straight ahead. There were only, for the next five minutes or so, two people in that room – Michael Meacher and myself. I began.

"Good evening, Minister. My name is John Moran, the local milkman. I have 600 customers in our village, I know them all, the different generations. I have lived in this village for over 20 years, I know the fears and I know what the people of our village are thinking. Tonight I come here on behalf of RASP as their Press Officer. I want to talk to you about what the SARP owners and management didn't discuss with you on your visit to their plant this afternoon." He looked a little bemused, the rest of those present more so. The elected councillors did not, however; they knew not to underestimate RASP, and they were right not to do so now.

"I could talk about the leaked documents, internal memos, site reports, letters confirming appalling work practices, pages of complaints to the Environment Agency, but as much as I would like that there is another matter that I would like to bring to your attention." I looked across at Michael Meacher and then continued, "When you visited the site this afternoon, we know you looked at the site, the incinerator, that you stood on top of the huge green storage tanks where you could hear the sounds of the children playing football on the school field close by, that you inspected the huge stockpiles of 15,000 drums on the site. We know all that, but the question I would ask you…" I slowly removed the envelope from my inside pocket, delivered earlier that day.

"Did they show you the rocket fuel?" I waited just a moment, just long enough for the impact of what I had said to sink in. "No, they wouldn't have shown you that, because they have got it buried under a soil bank covered by tarpaulins. There are 184 drums of an original consignment of 1,400 drums that they have had on site since 1995. They contain the flammable liquid UDMH, which we believe is the fuel of the Titan rocket. The drums, according to my source, are leaking and corroded. The good news is that you can't ignite the stuff with a spark or a naked flame, the bad news is that it can be ignited by another chemical. Nitric acid will do the job as good as anything else, the same nitric acid clouds that floated over our village on two days in May. I would like to assure you, Minister, and everyone here tonight that the situation is under control; my wife alerted the Environment Agency prior to this meeting and four of your officers are on site as we speak. The location of the drums has been found, the emergency services are on standby at the site, members of RASP are at the site observing."

Michael Meacher was visibly shaken by the latest revelations. I folded the letter, putting it back inside my pocket. I had done as I had been asked, I had delivered the message. Rising to his feet, the Minister of the Environment for the Labour government made his way outside to speak to the waiting crowds.

"I have come here today on a fact-finding mission, obviously I am very concerned. This plant, which deals in highly dangerous toxic wastes, has been subject to two serious incidents in May about a fortnight apart and has caused widespread public concern. I have also been presented by RASP many internal documents that raise grave concerns about the operations, management and safety of the plant. I want to thank all of the elected officials for their help in this matter, and to say how moved I was by the dignity with which the residents represented by Residents Against SARP Pollution put forward their case on behalf of the community. I will finish and leave you with this message – I rule nothing in and nothing out. I am going back to London to give this situation considerable thought."

He then turned and made his way to his waiting car. His vehicle was followed by several more cars containing the people who had been in the meeting, we were to say our goodbyes and farewell to him as he boarded the London train from Chesterfield. He shook hands with all who had been at the meeting and and the last I saw of him he was striding down the platform, briefcase under his right arm, towards the front first-class compartment, the packed train of commuters wondering who the guy was who had just passed them who had held them up for 15 minutes. The stationmaster closed the door behind the last passenger to board the 8.25 pm to London, blew his whistle and the train glided away.

That night I returned to the SARP plant a little over half an hour after seeing our visitor off. The RASP protesters were there in force, the revelation of the rocket fuel having been heard by hundreds outside the Village Centre over the relayed outside broadcast. Emergency services were still there, as were lots of SARP personnel running round in hard hats and protective clothing. The media were also there in numbers: local radio stations from Chesterfield and Sheffield, TV news reporters, camera crews, and newspapers like *The Sheffield Star* and *The Yorkshire Post*. Nicola Smith from *The Derbyshire Time*s led the questions.

"John, how did RASP get to know about this rocket fuel? Nobody, not even the Environment Agency, were aware of its presence."

"RASP was made aware of these barrels by someone who was concerned about his children and the danger that they were in."

"He must have been an employee to know so much," Nicola responded.

"I would not confirm or deny that, because I never asked. What I would like to add is that they have 15,000 drums on this site. If the unthinkable had happened and the orange nitric clouds released last May had landed on the corroded drums, then the ensuing secondary explosions in the close proximity of this huge stockpile would have been comparable with some of the major chemical disasters of the last 25 years. Flixborough, 1974, explosion killed 28, hundreds injured, and worst of all Bhopal, India, 1984, poison gas escaped from pesticides, more than 2,000 died. No, RASP will never be able to repay the debt of gratitude to people like my visitor this afternoon."

The next day the headlines said it all. "Rocket Fuel Uncovered at Waste Plant." The SARP UK plant was lurching from one disaster to another and it didn't matter how hard the PR company tried, they could not find a way to dampen it down. We were determined that our onslaught would continue.

That night at around 10.30 pm we were joined by Alan Charles. He had been invited into the SARP site by the Environment Agency to issue a statement to the residents waiting outside. He emerged and with the help of the now familiar loudhailer spoke to the waiting crowd. "The 184 remaining barrels of UDMH, known as 'rocket fuel' have been submerged under water to keep them stable; this is the correct way to keep them stored. They are going to be diluted and then removed from the site. They had apparently until last week stood in the open, uncovered, exposed to the elements, they were only buried a few days before the arrival of Mr. Meacher."

The next morning the Toxic Night Shift was about to make life harder for SARP.

"Can you come down to the gates, John? We have almost been overcome with fumes from the site. We have got the EA down again." It was Allison Sampson. My first thoughts were that the EA must have been back on site within hours of their colleagues leaving the previous night.

"What they are saying is they have a problem with the oil scrubbers," Allison added. To most of us not conversant with these terms, 'oil scrubbers' were, in Ian Legge's words, 'a device utilising a liquid designed to separate particulate matter or gaseous contaminants from a gas stream by one or more mechanisms' and if that's what our technical expert said, that was good enough for me. The one thing I did know was that the odours were horrendous.

The EA officers later emerged and said as they passed the waiting protesters, "The Environment Agency will be issuing a statement later today, at the moment we cannot comment."

That night the *Sheffield Star* headline screamed "SARP IN TROUBLE WITH THE ENVIRONMENT AGENCY". The article said: "For the third time in as many days the plant has been the subject of EA investigations and has now had the last remaining working process suspended. The EA reported: 'The secondary liquid fuel plant for the blending of solvents for fuel to industry was found to have major problems with the "oil scrubbers" that in turn was causing the release of toxic fumes. In the interests of the safety of the general public we have shut down SARP UK until we are satisfied that the oil scrubbers have been replaced and come up to the standard we expect from them.'"

They didn't bother to add that if it hadn't been for the Toxic Night Shift, one more smell, one more illegal emission, one more logged complaint would have joined the long list in their log described as "Unsolved residents' phone calls".

There were so many incidents happening at this waste plant that it was getting to the stage that sometimes I was delaying information about the 'errors' as we had stories overlapping. We were in "information overload" mode, it seemed, and thanks to SARP UK's complete incompetence it would go on for a while yet.

Monday as usual found us at the Crown. It seemed a long time ago in our lives when Monday was a free night. The commitment was as strong as ever – there were about 50 really dedicated protesters in RASP, at every meeting, every protest, every event these 50 were never missing, and tonight as I looked around the Crown they were all there.

The Chair was Wendy Wellings. She began, "Well, what is there to say about last week? Where do I begin? So much happened in our campaign. I would first congratulate our four speakers who spoke on behalf of RASP to Michael Meacher, we all heard you over the loudspeaker system. I thought you were all quite brilliant, we certainly have some very good speakers in our group. Secondly, well done to the Toxic Night Shift. I know you rotate, but Allison Sampson, Sandra Moran, Ann Cockerill, Ann Nettleship and June Cullabine last week had this company reeling. Firstly the toxic sludge, then the SLF plant shut down with the failure of the oil scrubbers. The EA must be nearly as fed up of you as SARP are. Alistair, have you anything planned for the coming week?"

Alastair replied, "We seem to be holding protests at random now, at least two 'gate protests' a week, the telephone tree makes it possible to organise a protest of at least 40 protesters within hours, we shall keep this going, and with the Toxic Night Shift working so well there is nothing that happens on site or even off it for that matter that we don't know about."

"Thank you, Alistair. Is there anything that anyone wishes to raise?" was Wendy's next question.

Terry Turner raised his hand. "I went down to the Parish Council meeting last week and they were discussing what they named 'The Killamarsh Environmental Enhancement Project'. There are plans to develop the Village Centre and Bridge Street using landfill tax from… you will never believe it – from SARP UK."

We were dumbfounded. Terry continued, "I have a newsletter that I picked up this morning, I shall read it to you all. 'Last year the Parish Council became aware of proposals by Leigh Environmental (now SARP UK) to use tax rebates from the Landfill Tax to redevelop the centre of the village, Bridge Street and the canal bridge area. The Government allows landfill operators to reclaim a tax credit of up to 90 percent of any donation to an Environmental Trust. Only landfill site operators can reclaim the tax. The donation can be made to nonprofit organisations, which cannot be a local authority or a corporate body controlled by one or more local authorities. This includes Parish, District and County Councils. Groundwork Cresswell has been appointed to plan the scheme and have used a £100,000 tax rebate [£90,000 from the tax, £10,000 from the Onyx Trust; this name just one of many that SARP UK shelter under]. In total £170,000 is being spent to enhance the Village Centre. Detailed proposals will be published soon and the public will be able to comment on the proposal.'"

Tony Ward was on his feet. "That is unbelievable, they know we are campaigning day and night to get this plant shut down and they are taking sweeteners from SARP!"

The whole room was in complete shock at Terry's news. Wendy was the next to respond. "When are they going to display the plans and invite the general public, does it say when, Terry?"

"No, but I think it will be in the next few weeks."

Wendy then responded, "In that case we have a few weeks, I am sure a lot of you here will be keen to look at the proposals. It does say on the newsletter that the Parish Council welcomes comments from residents." With that, Wendy brought the meeting to a close. There were a lot of people that night who felt that a line had been drawn in the sand. Derbyshire County Council and our own Parish Council in particular had been very lukewarm in their support of RASP in our fight to close SARP UK. Were these proposals one of the reasons?

Wednesday was always a light day on the milk, having left double deliveries on the Tuesday. I had started to really enjoy my Wednesdays – only one job to do, a real treat. The phone rang. It was Steve Martin. "John, you are not going to believe this." How many times had I heard that one lately? "SARP are being threatened with prosecution by Yorkshire Water."

"Where did you get that information, Steve?" I asked. Throughout this campaign we had never gone to the media unless we were 100 percent certain that it was correct; we knew one mistake and SARP would destroy us. Up to now that had not happened, and we were determined that we would avoid that situation at all costs.

"The bloke I know who is a driver for Yorkshire Water overheard his bosses talking, I am pretty certain it will be right."

"OK, Steve, I will follow it up – will let you know later," I replied. I placed the phone back on its receiver, and picking it up again I rang Yorkshire Water.

"Yorkshire Water, how can I help you?"

"Press Office here." I took care not to mention RASP.

"Oh yes, what can I do for you?"

At this apparent opening of the door I was not going to miss the opportunity. "Could you confirm that Yorkshire Water has told SARP UK at Killamarsh that it will take them to court?"

"Please hold the line, sir, I will put you through to someone who is involved in this operation." I heard her on the other phone say, "The press are on the phone about SARP UK and the intention to take them to court."

I just heard her colleague's response of, "How on earth did they get to know so quickly? We only decided an hour ago to write to SARP UK."

He then took the phone to speak to me. "Yes, sir, the information you have is correct, we have ordered SARP UK to close down an effluent pump. Following complaints about foul smells, Yorkshire Water has warned it will take legal action."

"Thank you," I mumbled, astonished at my apparent stroke of luck.

"What paper did you say you were from?" he asked.

"Oh, I am sorry – John Moran, Press Officer for the campaign group RASP." I replaced the receiver; minutes later the media were alerted.

The *Sheffield Star* headline that night was: "WASTE PLANT IN NEW STORM." Reporter Steve Caddy had written, "Owners of trouble-hit waste recycling plant have been threatened with prosecution for pollution. Yorkshire Water has told SARP UK management it will take them to court if effluent which pours from the plant into sewers at Killamarsh continues to break safety limits. The threat was revealed days after the Environment Agency ordered SARP to close down an effluent pump following complaints about foul smells.

"Yorkshire Water wrote to SARP directors after samples of effluent were found to contain too much solvent and other chemicals. The findings contradicted SARP's own analysis. The company was warned that from August 1 weekly samples would be taken and the first time one failed effluent tests Yorkshire Water warned it would launch legal action. Yorkshire Water has since not been able to take any samples because SARP UK is now storing all effluent on site rather than discharging to the sewers in Killamarsh.

"'The company has decided to test the effluent on site before disposing of it and SARP now has two large tanks of contaminated water on the site,' said a YW spokesman. Alan Charles said the revelations provided further evidence that SARP UK were unfit to run the facility. 'These are the same two tanks that gave off an awful smell last weekend, which caused the Environment Agency to instruct SARP to close down a pump,' he said."

Chapter Ten

Follow the Money

It was August 13, just after 9.30 am, and the phone was ringing again. I had been considering trying to get an hour's sleep. I had caught a glimpse of myself in the mirror as I returned home that morning from the round. Pale and drawn, I had aged years these last months, days and nights without sleep, sunken eyes. Yes, the fight against SARP was taking its toll on us all. I picked up the phone.

"Alistair here, John. Tonight they are unveiling the plans for the Village Centre; I think we have to be there to make clear our opposition to what we see as toxic money."

"OK," was my response, "I will organise as many as I can, I will put the telephone tree in operation right away."

"That's great. Becky Fryer is having some posters done opposing the plans, we will have them around the village by tonight. That's about it then, I will see you tonight." With that he was gone.

I left home around 7.15, intending to walk the half-mile to the Village Centre, but the early light rain had now turned heavy. Sandra, having spent time doing her hair, did not want to appear at the meeting looking like a drowned rat, so we decided to go down in the car.

As we pulled into the Village Centre it was already pretty full; there was obviously plenty of interest in the plans on display. We went through the reception area, following the signs to the main hall. There, on large display boards, were the artists' impressions of the village, with a flowered area, planted trees, benches and flagged areas; there were also some pictures of improvements to transform the Bridge Street pavement area with similar flowered areas, tree planting and street furniture.

Groundwork Cresswell were the organisation that had the contract to do the work and they were represented by Chris Mosley. I didn't know him, but I knew his mother, who was a receptionist at the local medical centre. On the table opposite were our Parish Councillors, John Holden, Jayne Holden, Grant Laughton and former Chairman Colin Robinson, who had been on this Council many years; a former National Coal Board official, he had run this Labour Council with an iron fist and his influence was deeply ingrained in all our Parish Council. Colin was a big man, round-faced, he was already mixing with the public, pointing at the displays with the odd laugh – he obviously wanted these improvements and wasn't too bothered who funded them.

By 8.15 the hall was full. A quick scan of the faces in the room told me that I was not on my own; in amongst the crowd were lots of familiar faces. RASP were always there, always at your back when they were asked. Colin Williams and his daughter Samantha, Brian and Margaret Ashmore, Brian without his beloved black beret – that's a first, I thought – Terry and May Hobson, Ian Legge, our technical expert, Alistair, his friend Steve Birch and Becky Fryer.

At just after 8.20 pm, the Parish Council, led by Colin Robinson, climbed the small steps that led to the main stage at the top of the hall. There were five chairs behind a long table that held five lonely looking microphones. Colin Robinson opened proceedings.

"The Killamarsh Parish Council welcomes you all here tonight, we are delighted to see so many of you taking such interest in our village. The Council would invite you now to ask us any questions and if you have any comments on the proposals."

Several people over the next half an hour asked questions of the councillors and Chris Mosley from

Groundwork Cresswell, who had now joined the others on the main stage.

"What is the timespan that this work will take?" one person asked.

"How will it disrupt my business?" one Bridge Street trader wanted to know.

"What effect will it have on the car parks?" asked another.

The councillors as ever were nothing if not smart, they were keeping everyone happy, as the public seemed to have had their say. The looks of a job well done were starting to cross the faces of the occupants of the top table. I was standing near to the front but to the left of the stage, where there were no steps. Many years on the milk had taught me how to scale obstacles of similar height in the early mornings when I thought that no one was watching, a practice I now frowned upon if any of my milk lads tried to emulate the feat. I moved quickly towards the stage and within seconds I had the end microphone in my hand. The look on Lady Jayne's face was disbelief, likewise Colin Robinson's – in all his many years he had never seen anyone challenge him in this village over parish council business.

I launched into full flow. "You have all looked at the plans, you have all looked at the flowers and the trees, you have all asked about the timespan to complete it, the effect it will have on your business; the question no one has asked is, 'Where is the money coming from?' Well, let's get that clear." I looked towards Colin Robinson, the next five seconds were taken up by silence. "No one wants to answer that. SARP. The same SARP UK that's poisoned and polluted us for the last 20 years, the same SARP UK that tried their best through incompetence – and are still trying – to blow us to kingdom come. The same SARP UK the campaign group RASP have been fighting all the way from Ellisons Road to the heart of Paris, and you, our Killamarsh Parish Council who are supposed to be with us..." looking towards the seated councillors, I continued, "you are wanting to take the toxic money. We at RASP say, 'We don't want toxic money, we want fresh air to breathe, fresh air for Killamarsh!'"

The scene was now mayhem, the elected officials, with the exception of Colin Robinson, had fled the stage, the unwelcome guest with the microphone had seen to that. Colin Robinson was sat on the front of the stage, head in hands. As I passed him on the way down, I spoke so only he could hear, "Never mind, Colin, you will fight back."

The next morning when I delivered the milk to the Village Centre, there was a note in the bottle. "The Killamarsh Parish Council no longer requires a milk delivery." It seemed that the fightback had already started.

I had only been back home that Tuesday morning a short time when the phone rang. "This is the BBC in London,

I am from the BBC Five Live programme *Hayes on Sunday* and we would like to come and do a program on your fight against toxic waste company SARP UK. We want to come to Killamarsh but we want it to go out this Sunday 16."

"No, that will be no problem, how many people would you like to meet from RASP?"

"About four or five, that will do nicely. Shall we say midday Wednesday?"

"That will be fine." With that the call ended.

I now had to contact the RASP members I thought would come over well in the recording. Ann Nettleship, Ann Cockerill, Sandra my wife and Carol Dye. They were my choice.

On Wednesday at midday the five of us were sitting waiting in my lounge when a knock at the door announced the arrival of the *Hayes on Five* team. The young lady leading the team and hosting the program was quite distinctive looking with her jet-black hair, ruby-red lips and odd dress sense. She introduced herself as Magenta Devine – we were not likely to forget her. Over the next hour or so she did interviews with us all, Ann Nettleship was particularly articulate as usual, Ann Cockerill and Sandra plenty feisty enough and Carol Dye on her best behaviour, no four-letter words today, thanks, Carol.

The interview over, Magenta wanted to see for herself how close the school was to the SARP plant, so we showed her the view from Wales Bar, the village that stands high on the hill on the Rotherham Road a mile beyond the Rother Valley Country Park entrance. This done, she asked to be taken to SARP UK, where she was to do an interview with Mark Stanley, head of the PR company employed by the French owners. We all looked forward to the Sunday night broadcast.

I had just finished doing my weekly milk accounts at about 5.30 pm, when the phone rang.

"Steve Martin here, John, can't stay on long, I'm on my mobile. I'm up near ICI on Teeside, I have just been with a guy in the transport café, and he tells me that the A1 at Foston has been closed. He reckons there was a green and white tanker involved, he thought it was a SARP tanker, could you check it out?"

"Will do, Steve." The mobile went dead.

I replaced my phone and then redialled. The voice on the other end answered, "*Sheffield Star* news desk, can I help?"

"Steve Caddy or Bill Brotherton, please."

"One moment, who should I say is speaking?"

"John Moran, Press Officer for RASP." The job description flowed easily; what once felt strange had become now a part of my everyday vocabulary.

"Bill Brotherton speaking. What was it, John, not another leak at SARP, surely not?"

"I think you may have got that right in one, Bill. Can you enquire of the Environment Agency if there has been an incident involving a SARP UK tanker at Foston on the A1?"

"Thanks, John, will do that right away."

The Sheffield Star ran the story: "SARP TANKER CLOSES A1."

Bill wrote, "A SARP UK tanker was spotted leaking its strong acid cargo whilst driving along the A1 at Foston. A concerned motorist managed to flag down the oblivious driver to alert him of the trail of leaking acid. The leak started at 4.00 pm and required eight fire engines and two ambulances at the scene. The emergency services were occupied for four hours and the road was closed for several hours.

"Foston is on the border of Lincolnshire and Nottinghamshire. The tanker was transporting 20 tonnes of Di-Hyroxy-Di-Pnenyl sulphate 2.5, which had to be transferred to another tanker. It was the failure of a rubber seal in one of SARP's tankers which caused the first of the two acid leaks in Killamarsh on that day back in May. John Moran, spokesman for RASP, said after hearing the news of the latest incident from this beleaguered company, 'It is clear that the lessons of the past have not been learned at SARP. The one question we don't have the answer to is, was there an acid cloud?'"

After the protest against the Parish Council's plans to accept the "toxic money" on the previous Monday, we had posters on every lamppost and noticeboard in the village, or so it seemed.

RESIDENTS AGAINST SARP POLLUTION SAY,
WE DON'T WANT YOUR TOXIC MONEY
Onyx Environmental Trust is a front organisation for SARP
Onyx is another waste management trust co in the same group as SARP, owned by multinational Vivendi.
This environmental trust is an attempt to persuade us that SARP has the interest of the environment and the local community at heart.
WE KNOW DIFFERENT!
How can we trust SARP following the two major emergencies in May and years of leaks, spills and smells, when they also hide rocket fuel on site?
WE WANT SARP OUT OF KILLAMARSH !
We don't want their dirty money, their toxic money.
Local councillors have supported our campaign so far, they must not accept money from SARP when we are campaigning to close them down, to accept the money could be seen as compromising their position.
Councillors have argued that SARP's continued operations are jeopardising regeneration in this area, we agree. There

can be no regeneration of the precinct with a toxic cloud hanging over us, at the very least let the people of Killamarsh decide.

The Council should organise a local referendum.

Do you want SARP to close its Killamarsh plant?

Do you want the Council to accept money from the Onyx Trust?

That night the Killamarsh Parish Council issued a press statement: "We have the offer from Onyx Trust, the improvements will go ahead. Groundwork Cresswell's Chris Mosley was pleased the work would go ahead and said, 'The intention was to start the end of September and I look forward to the challenge.' Bob Harper, speaking on behalf of the Parish Council, said: 'We thought long and hard about taking the money, but on balance we felt as the residents had suffered for all these years, they deserved something in return.'"

A spokesman for the campaign group RASP, in reply to Julia Lockwood on Yorkshire ITV Calendar News the following day, said: "We at RASP are extremely disappointed, we had asked for a referendum to let the people of Killamarsh decide. The Parish Council by their actions have made it clear where they stand. RASP is now on its own, the fight to close SARP UK rests with us. The residents of

Killamarsh should continue to support us, we will not let them down."

Sunday night found most of RASP at my house, as we had a decent-sized patio and front garden it didn't pose much of a problem. As Sandra kept up to 30 or more glasses and cups filled up with the help of Faye, we waited for the BBC Five Live broadcast to begin.

Magenta Devine gave a brief history to the background to the story, covering the experiences of people over the last 20 years, and how two days in May had resulted in RASP being formed. How we had protested at SARP day and night, marched down the Champs-Élysées in Paris. The way the four speakers from RASP put their cases on the programme was articulate and passionate, most impressive.

The response from SARP UK, care of Mr. Mark Stanley, was in complete contrast. Having to defend a company from incident after incident, from toxic sludge to leaking tankers, decaying tanks splitting in two and lastly storing fuel for Titan rockets and NASA space shuttles, as Magenta Devine put it, "Within earshot of the children playing out at playtime."

Mark Stanley, PR man for SARP UK, was having a most uncomfortable time, it must have been with a sense of relief he heard the words, "This is Magenta Devine for *Hayes on Sunday*, in a small village in North East Derbyshire that continues to take on the might of the French multinational Vivendi. I return you to the studio in London."

Two days later, on August 18, a reliable source informed us that the following had appeared pinned to the SARP UK internal noticeboard:

RASP

RESIDENTS AGAINST SARP POLLUTION

To Mr. Mark Stanley

Media Spokesperson & Director SARP UK

August 18, 1998

Dear Mr. Stanley,

Having heard with great interest your broadcast on the BBC Five Live program *Hayes on Sunday* on August 16, 1998, we wish to thank you for your communicative skills in this, a further effort by a SARP employee to ensure the fast demise of SARP UK on the Killamarsh site.

The RASP committee have held a special meeting and have voted to offer you a lifetime honorary membership of RASP, the action against SARP and this will cover all our usual membership benefits. These include a relocation allowance and removal expenses, free medical health plan and insurance protection. Legal representation is also provided to members. In your case, for the likely event that you will be called to answer for your poor performance on this broadcast by your managing director, this could be a distinct advantage.

Be assured that RASP looks after its members and we pride ourselves on our professional approach to our single objective to remove SARP UK from Killamarsh. We can offer you retraining in media coverage and if you are successful we will offer a suitable executive role.

Thanking you once again for your determined effort to aid our cause,

We remain sincerely yours

The RASP action group.

Chapter Eleven

TNT and the Toxic Package

On the Monday, August 17, I was at my last call of the morning at around 8.15 am. This last call was the supermarket on Delves Road on the White City; I was in the back of the shop filling up the fridge when a young man in his late twenties stopped to speak to me. "Are you John Moran from RASP?"

"I am, how can I help you?" I asked.

"Ask TNT what happened to the driver taking a package to Wilton in the North East." He turned and was gone, I never had time to see his face – maybe that was just the way he wanted it to be. Intrigued, I knew that TNT parcel vans were seen leaving SARP; this had to be to do with SARP, but how could I find out? I knew TNT would be reluctant to talk to me. John Moran, Press Officer, RASP, was hardly likely to get the story.

I rang Graham Readfearn on *The Yorkshire Post*. Graham was, I thought, a good reporter – he had done some great reports about RASP and had been reporting our campaign since the beginning.

"Will you do me a favour, Graham?" I asked.

"If I can, John – what is it?"

"Will you ring TNT, the parcel couriers, and ask them what happened to the driver taking the package to Wilton in the North East? You may just get a story."

The next morning the headline in *The Yorkshire Post* read: "UNMARKED WASTE POLLUTED COURIER VAN". Graham had got the exclusive.

"The owners of an industrial waste plant came under fire again last night after it was revealed that a package of hazardous waste had leaked and contaminated a courier van. The courier firm TNT confirmed it was co-operating with Health and Safety Executive officers after a package from SARP UK's Killamarsh plant near Rotherham leaked during transit.

"Campaigners battling for the closure of the plant said it seemed the firm could not even be trusted to wrap a parcel, and local MP Harry Barnes described the incident as disturbing. TNT said SARP had breached carriage guidelines by failing to tell them the package contained hazardous material, and said they were holding the company liable for the problems.

"A spokesman for SARP UK said last night the firm was not in a position to comment about the incident but a statement would be released today. TNT said last night the package was picked up from Killamarsh on August 5, but leaked in the later stages of its journey, in the Durham area. Only then did staff realise the material was hazardous and had created a contamination risk. A spokesman said, 'Unfortunately SARP staff neglected to inform us of the contents, did not affix a Hazchem label and did not protect the contents sufficiently against leakage. TNT is holding SARP liable for the problems which have been caused and we are co-operating fully with investigations by the Health and Safety Executive.'

"The spokesman said the firm's condition of carriage clearly stated that customers were responsible for declaring the contents of any hazardous consignments. John Moran, a spokesman for Residents Against SARP Pollution said, 'SARP clearly can't be trusted to even wrap a parcel. More appalling work practices have now come to light, but we are not surprised in the least to hear this news, and the fact that the driver of the TNT van had to be rushed to hospital with breathing difficulties, people in Killamarsh know exactly how he felt, they too have the same problem. We at RASP think it is unbelievable that these incidents keep going off and they keep getting let off the hook. The number of investigations there seems to be unreal.' North Derbyshire MP Harry Barnes said, 'It's very disturbing and the full facts need to be investigated as soon as possible. It's an extra matter of concern that the problems at the Killamarsh plant now seem to be being exported elsewhere.'"

Two days later, the PR company posted a letter on its internal noticeboard at SARP UK.

INTERNAL COMMUNICATION
(Strictly for Internal Use Only)
FOR IMMEDIATE RELEASE ON ALL NOTICEBOARDS

INCIDENT INVOLVING CARRIAGE OF A WASTE SAMPLE

On August 5, 1998, a waste sample which was being carried by the parcel company TNT leaked in transit, resulting in a potential risk that other parcels in the vehicle could have been contaminated.

The sample was on route from Killamarsh to our Wilton site office. The company liaised with TNT to contact organisations that had received parcel deliveries that day to advise them of our concern and the potential risk so they could inspect their packages and decide what course of action was appropriate if they suspected any of their items were affected.

We confirm that nobody was injured as a result of this incident and that a thorough investigation is being conducted within SARP and by the carrier TNT and both companies are liaising with the Health and Safety Executive.

NB Following the incidents at Killamarsh in May, there is a high level of external and media interest in our Killamarsh operation and our activities in general and this regrettable incident will be widely reported.

We must all appreciate that our activities for the foreseeable future will be subject to a high level of public scrutiny and any minor mistakes or oversights are likely to be expanded and heavily reported.

It is important that all of us are extremely vigilant to ensure that our methods of operation and procedures are followed and attention to detail is critical.

If you require any further information on the above, please contact my office.

Mr. Stanley 20.08.98.

Another bad day at the office for Mr. Stanley. At £10,000 per week, he and his PR company were looking a little overpaid, but in his defence, as Alistair once told me, "SARP UK are trying to defend a lie, we only have to tell the truth."

Mark Stanley resigned later that day by mutual consent.

Chapter Twelve

The Day the Grim Reaper Came to Call

RASP for a long time had been pressing and lobbying for an early warning siren at the SARP UK site. The installation of this, we felt, was justified because, firstly, any time gained by the community in the event of a major incident had to be a good thing and, secondly, that the very presence of such an early warning siren would bring attention to the danger on our doorstep. At SARP UK they were smart enough to have figured that out for themselves, and up to now had resisted the calls for such a system. However, in an act of desperation following the recent spate of bad publicity, they had decided to agree to the demands of the community and prepare to install the system, but they first had to carry out tests to see if it worked. They knew they were taking a risk, but as we knew of old they were experts in "risk assessments" – that had always been one of their problems as it had for many years previously under their other name Leigh Environmental.

Martin Frobisher, the Site Manager, issued the following press statement: "SARP UK, in conjunction with the Derbyshire County Council, announce that we have installed an early warning siren to alert the general public. The siren will be heard up to a two-mile radius, and we will be testing this on Thursday August 20 at 7.00 am, 11.00 am and lastly at 7.00 pm. It will have a two-tone sound. The installation of this siren confirms our commitment to the local community and furthers our aims at SARP UK to be seen as good neighbours."

Martin Frobisher and SARP UK knew that this could backfire. How RASP would react this would be key; they were to soon find out.

Monday night in the Crown, after the usual preliminaries, Kevin turned to Alistair. "What plans have we for the coming week?"

"Today, as you all know, SARP UK announced the testing of an early warning system. Although we in principle welcome it, it in no way helps us shut this place down. We know that they are hurting financially, only three of their original processes are being allowed to operate. They are desperate to get the incinerator up and running. This siren, if a success, will, they feel, be a step to achieving that. What response should RASP take in order that we turn this round to help our cause, not theirs?"

"Well, we should hold protests to coincide with the three tests," said Brian Ashmore.

"What we should do is hold one at the SARP gates, preferably the 7.00 am testing, the 11.00 am at the Rother Valley Country Park and the 7.00 pm one in the village. But if it is to have more effect we should all fall to the ground and 'play dead' – that will suggest the warning has failed and the aftermath," said Alistair. "We will organise the three protests, can you all use the telephone tree and alert as many as you can?"

It was Thursday August 21, 6.45 am. I had started the milk round early, finished for a little after 6.30 am. I turned the corner in my milk van and drove the 250 yards from my unit to the gates of SARP UK. Alistair, Carol Dye, Brian and Margaret Ashmore, Terry and May Hobson, Steve Birch, Dave Milson… the usual suspects were all there. Standing a little detached from the main group, either by chance or design, was the dark figure of the Grim Reaper, scythe in hand.

We all waited, and at the stroke of 7.00 am the sound of the siren broke the silence in a two-tone wail. 150 people fell to the ground, they fell where they had been standing, banners and placards still in hand. In the eerie silence that followed, the only movement was the figure of the Grim Reaper as he walked amongst the "dead". The media was having a field day – TV and radio and all the press had been alerted.

A similar scenario repeated itself at 11.00 am in the Rother Valley down at the visitors' centre, where around 100 or so protesters blocked all roads in. As the park has 750,000 visitors per year, the chaos can be imagined. The only thing wrong was that no one heard the siren. The third and final testing was at 7.00 pm. RASP had arranged to assemble near the corner of Sheffield Road and Bridge Street, the busiest junction in our village. At 6.45 pm the best part of 200 people walked into the road, traffic came to a halt as the first protesters had used the zebra crossing, meaning all traffic had to give way. At 6.58 pm the protesters stood silently blocking the roads, banners and placards held in front of them, the Martin girls with their now famous RASP banner that had chased Vivendi halfway round Europe. On the stroke of 7.00, to what could only have been described as a murmur from the siren, the protesters all over the busy junction dropped to the ground for the third time that day. They lay as before all over the road, placards and banners at their sides, only the Grim Reaper upright and wandering amongst them. As we lay there, the silence was eerie; it was later likened to a misty November Remembrance Sunday when the minute's silence is observed, only in this case it was at least five minutes. The silence was broken by Kevin Jones, our RASP Chairman, who leapt to his feet and, producing a klaxon horn, did two long blasts on it, commenting, "We knew that SARP wouldn't get it right so we decided to bring our own."

In hindsight it was very funny, but in reality it was scary: once again SARP UK had proved how incompetent they were.

The front page of *The Sheffield Star* featured a half-page colour photograph of all the protesters lying across the Sheffield Road, bodies everywhere, with the headline, "THE DAY THE GRIM REAPER CAME TO CALL".

The next day another headline was: "'Barely audible' siren slammed." The article went on to say: "Tests of the warning siren installed at the Killamarsh plant of SARP UK have been slammed by the community. The two-toned siren, designed to be heard two miles away, was barely audible at the Parkside shopping centre in the centre of the town. Protesters claimed that it was drowned out by passing shopping trolleys, and others said they had heard nothing at all. The siren was installed in response to the confusion that existed when there were two leaks of toxic gas from the plant earlier this year. In a letter to residents, SARP UK had advised that the siren would be a signal for residents to stay indoors, close all the windows and listen to local radio stations for information. Three tests were conducted yesterday, Thursday. Anyone wishing to comment on the siren's effectiveness is invited to contact the company on a special hotline number."

The hotline was suspended just after midday on the Friday – it had been open for less than three hours. Another disastrous 24 hours in the life of SARP UK and, although they didn't know it, things were not going to get any better in the foreseeable future.

In a Yorkshire ITV press conference outside the SARP gates, I was asked, "What is your response to the early warning siren that SARP UK tested yesterday?"

"RASP's response is early warning sirens are a good idea. RASP's fears are that we don't trust the person with his finger on the button. Time will show that they will, when faced with a serious incident on this site, fail to sound it – it would be admission of another failure."

Humour had only ever been just below the surface in this campaign. It has raised its head on many occasions, only to be submerged by the fight to close SARP UK. The relief at being able to have a laugh (usually at the expense of SARP UK) had kept us going through the intensity of the campaign. The phone call I got on August 24 was about to reveal the latest cause for humour to raise its head.

"Mike Sampson here, John." A RASP member from the beginning, Mike was Kevin Sampson's father; he lived at nearby Kiveton Park and was one of the key figures in the RASP branch there.

"What can I do for you, Mike? I don't often get phone calls from you."

"I've just heard a funny story, I'm sure you'll like it. This morning on the SARP UK site a chemist was working on the top of a tanker, he had a safety harness on and was fastened to the tanker, fixing tamper-tags to the top of it. The driver thought everything was completed – I think you could call it a lack of communication, whatever – the driver starts to drive off, oblivious of the terrified chemist clutching the top of his tanker. As he passed the admin block, the chemist removes his safety helmet and throws it at the windows, this alerts office staff who, on leaping from their desks and rushing to the windows, were just in time to see the tanker reaching the end of Ellisons Road, about to turn left in the direction of the M1."

That night the media, as they like to say at SARP UK, reported it heavily. The headlines in all the papers were "TANKER DRIVES OFF WITH MAN STILL ON ROOF". I am afraid that the story in the retelling grew slightly: reports of the terrified chemist on the M1 halfway to Leeds were greatly exaggerated; in fact a passing motorist flagged the oblivious tanker driver to a halt just past the entrance to the Rother Valley Country Park, to the eternal thanks of one harness-clad chemist, who was last seen walking sheepishly but unhurt back down Ellisons Road.

On the morning of August 26, I would rather not say from whom, I was given a fax. It had been sent to SARP UK in Killamarsh from the SARP office in Deeside, and read:

"From Craig Wilson. 20-8-98. With reference to my fax sent to 'X' concerning disposal of effluent solids from ICI Polyurethanes containing total chlorinated material 1000ppm, X confirmed to me that he could dispose of the material at £17 per tonne. This waste (three tipper wagons) will arrive on Wednesday next week."

My mole informed me that when the three tippers arrived at the site that morning, the landfill on the site run by the sister company Onyx was there to receive them. According to the licensing conditions governing the landfill site, only five percent liquid to 95 percent solid is permitted. The mole told me that when tipped it was more liquid than solid – clearly a flagrant breach of the licence. The headlines appeared that night and the next day in *The Yorkshire Post*.

"ENVIRONMENT AGENCY BEGINS INVESTIGATION AFTER FRESH ALLEGATIONS; INQUIRY INTO ILLEGAL WASTE DUMPING AT TOXIC DUMP". The story, by Rob Waugh, ran: "The Environment Agency last night confirmed it had launched an investigation into allegations that a consignment of waste had been illegally dumped at a landfill site adjacent to the controversial SARP UK plant in Killamarsh. A spokesman said the allegations were of a serious nature and, if proved to be true, would represent a major breach of the waste management licence held by Onyx Landfill Ltd, a sister company of SARP UK. *The Yorkshire Post* understands that the investigation will also involve claims that an inaccurate description of the waste was later filed in company documents.

"The inquiry will centre on a delivery of 24 tonnes of waste which arrived at the site on the outskirts of Sheffield in three tippers last Wednesday. The landfill is only licensed to take solid waste but it is alleged that most of the consignment was liquid chemicals, which were then illegally dumped. Neither SARP UK, whose Deeside plant had arranged the waste delivery, nor Onyx Landfill Ltd was available for comment last night. Both companies are part of the Onyx Leigh group but have separate waste management licenses. An Environment Agency spokeswoman said, 'An allegation was made and Agency inspectors went out to the site that night, and have started an investigation. They will be speaking to workers at the site, looking at paperwork and investigating what was put on the site. The Derbyshire County Councillor Alan Charles said the allegations were extremely worrying. Charles said, "If these allegations are true, it calls into question the integrity of the whole waste disposal industry. If this has happened while this company and its associates are under such scrutiny, you have to wonder what may have been dumped there in the past.' A spokesman for the pressure group Residents Against SARP Pollution, John Moran, said, 'We have been extremely concerned about the landfill site and the activities on it and have furnished information to the Environment Agency. We are pleased they are taking the issue seriously and look forward to their findings.'"

I didn't bother to add that I had been witness to the presence of two flat-back lorries arriving at this site in the very early hours every Tuesday morning for years. They parked up near the top of the site covered in weatherproof sheets, not revealing from where they came, until one of my milk lads scaled the perimeter fence, turned back the sheet, and revealed the name and address of the haulier, three miles from Sellafield nuclear power station in Cumbria, a round trip of 374 miles. The implications were now obvious.

The phone rang again just after 7.30 pm on August 27. "Can you get that, Faye, I'm in the shower?" I shouted out in the hope that someone would hear me.

"OK, Pops." The phone stopped ringing. "It's Ann Nettleship, her and June Cullabine are down at the gates. They say there is a lot of activity and can you go down?"

"15 minutes, I will be there." I heard Faye confirm the message, by that time I was almost dressed and on my way.

When I arrived I was met by around 20 protesters who were routinely making sure that everything was being run correctly at the site. SARP UK must have hated us, always there, always watching, always listening, always sniffing the air, now they were learning what was like to be unable to breathe.

"What's happening, Ann?" I asked.

"We are not quite sure, John, we have just seen Martin Frobisher, the Site Manager, and his Technical Manager Alan Timperley." Ann seemed to know the names and titles of all the site employees, I suppose she and June had spent so much time there they were part of the family, although on second thoughts "family" is definitely not the word that I was looking for.

"They both ran out of the admin block, we thought that they were in a liaison meeting with Alan Charles and the other councillors, but they had gas masks on and protective clothing. They ran up the site, I think that it is something to do with the rocket fuel."

Ann, as usual, had read it right. The media were alerted at 8.30 pm that evening and the message was left for Oliver Wright on the *Sheffield Star* news desk to contact the Environment Agency to enquire of the barrel of rocket fuel that had started to leak at approximately 7.35 pm.

The next day's headlines read: "ROCKET FUEL DANGER LEAK – ALERT SPARKS NEW SARP PLANT FEARS". Oliver had written: "Bosses at the controversial

SARP UK plant in Killamarsh today admitted that a barrel of high-explosive rocket fuel started leaking last night – sparking a major safety alert. The fire brigade were put on a state of high alert while workers at the plant contained the leak, which was spotted in a routine check yesterday evening. But an emergency siren warning local residents of possible danger was not sounded. It is the latest scare on the doorstep of hundreds of homes. And the *Star* understands that prosecutions could be brought against the company for previous safety breaches within a matter of weeks. A spokesman for the plant said this afternoon, 'SARP UK can confirm that its staff at Killamarsh treated a drum of rocket fuel that had developed a slight leak.

"'The leak was spotted during a routine investigation and management liaised with the fire brigade and the Environment Agency.' The spokesman said the contents of the drum were treated by putting it in water and they had not considered it necessary to warn residents. The leaking drum was one of almost 200 barrels of high-octane fuel which are at the waste site. News of the incident resulted in a demonstration outside SARP's gate. Experts have revealed the fuel should be kept submerged underwater but the barrels are being kept in dry storage while a water tank is built. John Moran, spokesman for the local pressure group RASP, expressed fury that warning sirens were not activated."

On September 1 RASP received a copy of a letter sent to Jean-Marie Messier, the President of Vivendi, from Alan Charles. This letter, as much as any I had seen in this campaign, emphasised the dangers that all of the residents in our village were facing from SARP UK.

Dear M. Messier,

Re: SARP UK Killamarsh

Clive Betts MP has passed me a copy of a letter that you have sent to him, dated July 29, 1998. In your letter you acknowledge that "the Killamarsh site has had a poor reputation within the community" and there is no reason why SARP Industries should not establish good relationships in Killamarsh.

Having read your letter I thought, as an elected representative of the Killamarsh community, I should explain, for your enlightenment, one or two reasons why SARP UK will never be able to establish good relationships with the residents of Killamarsh.

You were quite correct in your observation that the site had a poor reputation in the past, but the past pales into insignificance with the appalling record on the site since your company took over the responsibility for the operations on the site. The previous problems with the site predominantly centred around foul and obnoxious odours coming off the site on a frequent basis, often rising from the drains connected to the main sewer system within our main shopping area. SARP UK has done nothing to alleviate these problems despite repetitive promises to do so.

However, I need to inform you that since the two major leaks of nitric/sulphuric acid and nitric hydrofluoric acid gas clouds in May that brought fear, apprehension and extreme anger to my community, the self-induced reputation of your company has deteriorated beyond belief. Despite repeated statements to local representatives and the media that SARP UK operate a policy of total honesty, we find that you are only open and honest with the issues that you want the community to have knowledge of. There would appear to be new incidents happening every day that are connected to your Killamarsh site, most of which have been discovered by the residents' action committee, Residents Against SARP Pollution. Incidents exposed by RASP include the foul smelling sludge from Holder 18 that was left on the ground and not cleaned up, the blocked scrubber filters on the SLF process, the unmarked hazardous chemical (analyne) package that were sent by TNT Carriers to Teeside and leaked en route, endangering the driver and his assistant. The SARP UK tanker that leaked on the A1 en route from Leeds to Essex, the 'rocket fuel' that is stored on site that SARP never thought it necessary to inform local representatives of its existence, and the latest investigation by the Environment Agency into the alleged acceptance of material that did not conform with the licence on the Onyx landfill site at Killamarsh. Your company has spent a considerable amount of capital installing a warning siren, a project that has been labelled a total failure. It most certainly cannot be clearly heard in the village of Killamarsh, never mind the designed 2 km radius.

The most serious incident was last Thursday, August 27, at the liaison meeting. Members of the liaison committee watched a video of a site in the USA that produced one of the chemical compounds in rocket fuel. There was an accident at the site whereby the site in its entirety and everything else within a 1.5 km radius was totally destroyed. A television crew coincidentally was working in the area and caught the full horror on film. Martin Frobisher and Mark Stanley failed to inform the local representatives at that meeting that, whilst we were watching the video on your site at that very time, your operatives were frantically trying to deal with a drum of rocket fuel that was leaking and presumably causing serious concern, sufficient to warn the Fire and Rescue service to remain on standby. If this is the Vivendi meaning of "openness and honesty with the local community", you may well begin to understand why you will never enjoy any confidence whatsoever from my local community, indeed I believe it would be fair to say that the local community has no confidence at all in your company.

Finally, can I ask that your company cease its practise of referring to the residents of Killamarsh as "neighbours". My constituents find your use of this term to be extremely patronising, We associate the term "neighbour" with consideration and care for others in the vicinity, qualities that most certainly cannot be attributed to SARP UK or its holding company Vivendi. It is my firm belief that you as the Chairman of Vivendi should give serious consideration to your corporate responsibility and relocate this extremely poor, sub-standard plant to a site that is remote from schools, country parks and housing.

Yours sincerely,

Alan Charles

Derbyshire County Councillor.

The particular video that Alan Charles referred to had also been viewed by RASP. The film had shown the complete devastation around the PEPCON chemical plant in Nevada, USA, for a radius of 1.5 km, after a fire on May 4, 1988 ignited hundreds of barrels of ammonium perchlorate, a substance used in rocket fuel. We estimated if that happened at the Killamarsh site of SARP UK on a school day that both schools would have been destroyed and two thirds of the village. The expected death toll would have been 5,000 people, including hundreds of children. We were playing for high stakes. We could not afford to lose.

Sandra celebrated her 49th birthday on August 30, 1998, and about 35 friends had been invited for a party. I had asked my daughter Faye to pick up the present from Sheffield's

Cole Brothers, better known as John Lewis; I had been so busy these last months that shopping for birthday presents had not been at the top of my priorities. Faye also organised the party, her time as maître d' at Barnaby's in Los Angeles put to good use. Among the guests were lots of our fellow protesters from RASP who had become close friends, as well as Sandra's workmates from Derwent House, Chesterfield, the care home where she worked. Ann and Trevor Cockerill helped with the drinks, keeping everyone's glasses topped up.

The party went on till well into the early morning. Predictably the talk centred around the battle to close SARP UK; that was what we at RASP had become, we ate, slept and breathed it. That night there were two people there I had never seen at a SARP protest or a RASP meeting. They didn't get into the SARP conversation much but sat quietly in the corner. For reasons that I alone knew, a promise I made and still keep today, they could not be seen to be involved, but their contribution had been immeasurable.

The party had been a welcome relief, if only for a few hours, but the next day we were back down to business. At the meeting on the following Monday, Wendy Wellings was installed as our new Chairperson. Pressure of time and commitment had finally told on Kevin Jones, and he had found it impossible to run his business and spend the hours needed in the campaign. Wendy thanked him in his absence for all he had contributed to RASP and all the time he had given. We were all sorry to see him leave us, but we all knew the pressures, the hours without sleep, so it came as no surprise. There were many others who had packed it in with less prominent roles than Kevin. I suppose his going got to us a little more.

"Who is going to start?" Wendy's first words as Chair were answered by Alistair.

"I will. Firstly, we are organising a Three-Legged March for Saturday September 12. We leave the Kwik Save car park at 11.00 am, Wales and Kiveton leave at 11.00 am and Beighton will set off at 10.30 am. All three marches will rendezvous at the top of Ellisons Road at 12.00 midday. Then we all march on to the SARP gates. We have our leaflets – will everyone on leaving here tonight take 100 and please make sure that they leaflet their usual area. On other matters, I feel we should be starting new tactics against SARP, as we know that they have had major changes of personnel. They have sacked the PR company and installed another old Leigh man in Phil Rostance as spokesman for press releases and speaking to the media, they have replaced Martin Frobisher the Site Manager… at the moment we are not sure who the replacement will be, but more than likely another old Leigh man. We cannot blame them, it had to be expected that with so many incidents something had to change. That is why we are going to have to change as well. We have always been one step ahead and we will have to think of new things to try, as well as still using the old ones that have worked so well for us up to now. So I ask tonight for new ideas." Having opening the floor up for new suggestions, Alistair looked around the room.

"I think we should have a trip to Brownhills in Walsall, they are now SARP and I think that the French bosses might live in the area. We could make a surprise trip to their homes, that would be a nice surprise just after Sunday breakfast to see us lot arrive with our banners," said Carol Dye.

"I think that's a good idea, but no, I don't agree with visiting people's homes." David Parr was clearly against it.

"OK, we will put that idea on hold, but the first idea of the protest at Brownhills – I think that most of us would be up for that. We will try to arrange something."

Alistair was trying to calm things down. There were parts of the group who thought that there were no holds barred in this fight with SARP UK, and there were the less militant, like David Parr. The balance had been about right up to now: that was the reason the group had done so well. I must admit that both Sandra and myself favoured the Carol Dye mode of action – as Sandra reminded me, David Parr had been involved in the 1986 protest group and they had been too "nice". That way didn't work then and it wouldn't work now.

"Any more ideas?" Alistair asked once again.

"I think that we should start finding out who SARP do business with and first write to them, explaining our position, and if we get no response do a flying picket to their offices," said Steve Martin, who always had some good ideas.

"Yes, we will try to get hold of their supplier list and carry on from there," answered Alistair.

"I think that we should do a rooftop protest at SARP – that will definitely keep us in the spotlight. We will probably get arrested, but the court case will be an embarrassment to SARP," said Ann Cockerill.

"I would be up for that, who fancies coming up with me?" asked Alistair.

"I would come up with you." Everyone looked round to see who this very quiet voice had come from. It was Louise Wellings, the daughter of the Chairperson Wendy.

"Don't be ridiculous, Louise, you get dizzy when you stand on a chair, God knows what you would be like sat on the top of SARP's administration block," was all Wendy could say.

"I have two boys, seven and 10, they breathe those chemicals in day after day. We only live 100 yards from that incinerator. If I can't get over my nerves about heights for me, I will for them. I will go with you, Alistair, when the time comes."

I rose to my feet and started to clap and all the RASP members joined in, There was Louise, five feet nothing, seven stone nothing, terrified of heights, and she was going to hold a rooftop protest. With young people in the group like her, no wonder we were giving SARP a run for their money.

"Is there anything else before we close?" Wendy asked, still quite visibly shocked by her daughter's commitment to the rooftop protest.

"I have something I want to run by everyone," I said, rising to my feet again. "I think that in the light of the problems with the rocket fuel we should oppose the reopening of the two Sheffield Road schools. I propose we write to the Education Committee suggesting that the schools remain closed till SARP either disposes of or removes the remaining barrels of rocket fuel at the site. We have all seen the video evidence from the USA of what happens when this rocket fuel explodes, and we have had it confirmed today that there have been two other 'leaking barrel' incidents, making a total of three in the month of August at SARP."

Everyone agreed that I should do this, and with that Wendy brought the meeting to a close.

The next day I wrote the letter to Councillor Wilcox at Derbyshire County Council's Education Committee in Matlock.

Dear Sir,

In the light of the situation regarding SARP UK at Killamarsh over "rocket fuel" or 184 barrels of Dimethyl hydrazine, these are now known to have leaked and parents of children at the Sheffield Road Junior and Infant Schools have come to me to express their grave concern.

They request that you as Chair of the Education Committee use your powers to delay the return of all pupils to these two schools until these barrels have been incinerated or removed from the site. Nothing less, in the opinion of RASP, will be good enough for the safety of our children and grandchildren. The urgency of the situation cannot be expressed strongly enough and your intervention at the earliest is required.

John Moran,
Press Officer, RASP

We knew at RASP that the Education Committee was now faced with a dilemma. To delay the return of 500 schoolchildren would become front-page news in the national, not just the local media. The problem for Derbyshire County Council was that to close the schools would be an admittance of the dangers that the children were facing, but if they didn't close and something went badly wrong, which was highly likely knowing SARP UK's record, the consequences were unthinkable. To what degree politicians would gamble with people's lives would become evident in the weeks to come.

Before a decision had been made, the story had been picked up by Graham Readfearn at *The Yorkshire Post*. He wrote: "Children could be kept away from two village schools this week after parents expressed safety fears about rocket fuel being stored yards away at an industrial waste plant. Parents of children attending infant and junior schools at Killamarsh near Sheffield are demanding the fuel be removed from the SARP UK plant before their children return to school on Wednesday.

"But Derbyshire County Council said no decision would be made on whether it was safe for children to return until they had consulted environment and safety experts. SARP UK said yesterday they had completed intermediate storage plans by moving the barrels underwater, but claimed protestors had delayed plans by tampering with a standpipe being used to fill the lagoons.

"Father Darren Stanley, whose five-year-old, Jack, is due to start at the infant school on Wednesday, said, 'My worst fear is if that rocket fuel goes up, there will be no more Killamarsh and I will not see my child grow up. We are living in fear.'

"Playing fields at the junior school back directly on to the industrial waste plant currently under investigation for a series of toxic leaks. Fears were heightened last week when three of the barrels were found to have been leaking in the last month. Protest group RASP have written to the chairman of Derbyshire Education Authority, Councillor David Wilcox, asking him to 'delay the return of all pupils to these two schools until these barrels have been incinerated or removed.'

"Mr. Stanley, 30, of Sherwood Road, Killamarsh, said, 'I don't want Jack to go back, not until they have sorted it out. It is disgraceful having that plant here, so close to two schools, I am not letting him go until I am reassured it is safe. Kevin Sampson, whose daughter Charlotte is due back at the junior school on Wednesday, said, 'If that fuel goes up, it is bye-bye to that plant and the schools will go with it.'"

Despite this publicity, Derbyshire Education Authority took a chance – over 500 children were allowed back to school on the Wednesday.

September saw the RASP campaign carry on very much as before. We were having two or three early morning protests, resulting in blockades of the gates until the police come to clear us from the road. SARP had tightened the plant up now; of the original seven processes that they operated at the site prior to the May incidents, they had only managed to restart one – that was the SLF, the secondary liquid fuel plant. There were whisperings that they were very keen to restart their incinerator; this was the process more than anything that we at RASP wanted stopped, almost all of the pollution had been caused by this process and this was our biggest battle.

On Wednesday September 8, we had information from someone that worked at the Rother Valley Country Park that they were going to be issued with gas masks. At first I thought it was a windup, but he also told us that they were going to install a huge "water curtain". I rung Graham Readfearn at *The Yorkshire Post* to get him on the case, and the next day the following story appeared: "Safety Ideas Follow Leak from SARP Plant – Park May Issue Gas Masks After Acid Cloud Scare." Graham's article read: "Gas masks could be issued to staff at a country park after they breathed in toxic fumes during a gas leak from a nearby industrial waste plant. Other elaborate plans being discussed for staff and visitors at Rother Valley Country Park near Sheffield include a huge water curtain to take away toxic fumes and an escape plan. About six members of park staff suffered from breathing difficulties when an orange cloud of acid blew over the park on May 30. Rother Valley Country Park is one of the biggest attractions in the area, with 750,000 visitors every year. David Aspinall, Rotherham Borough Council countryside officer, said the gas masks and water curtain ideas had been discussed in meetings with officers from Derbyshire County Council. He said, 'I cannot expect staff to go into a pollution cloud without proper safety equipment. One member of staff was off for several days.' He understood a series of water jets creating a curtain could be set up in a position that could intercept any future gas clouds, taking the gas particles out of the air. A Derbyshire Council spokesman confirmed talks on water curtain ideas had taken place with emergency planning officers there.

"Kevin Barron, MP for Rother Valley, said, 'I think this whole debate is bizarre. The park and the nearby schools are not the problem, the problem is the SARP plant. I hope people concentrate their minds on that.' He said he would support any calls for a public enquiry into the activities at the plant.

"A spokesman for the action group RASP, John Moran, said it was ridiculous that people should be forced to take such measures, adding, 'We welcome anything that shows the dangers from that plant.' An announcement from the Health and Safety Executive and the Environment Agency into the first incident on May 14, when acid leaked from a tanker forcing villagers indoors, is expected within the next two weeks.

In the following week we made the papers again, this time in an article in *The Sheffield Star* dated September 14 and written by Steve Caddy, headlined "Protestors Ready to Risk Arrest." Steve wrote: "Campaigners are ready to be arrested as they try to turn tankers away from a controversial waste recycling plant. Organisers are hoping to attract up to 400 people to a protest rally at the gates of SARP UK at

Killamarsh tomorrow. They plan to turn back chemical tankers trying to get through to the plant despite the threat of arrest by the Derbyshire Police.

'"The police have told us they will arrest anyone who stops tankers going to SARP. But if any tankers do come down they will be stopped,' said John Moran of Residents Against SARP Pollution. 'We believe that getting this place shut down is more important than anything else. If that means getting arrested, then so be it.' Group members have repeatedly turned back tankers at past demonstrations without being arrested.

"Derbyshire Police Inspector Dick Severns was concerned about the dangers involved in stopping the vehicles. 'On occasions tankers have been held up when they are carrying potential hazardous substances,' he said. 'We are getting more and more of it. We have to draw a line and say it has got to stop. We can't allow people to obstruct the highway.'"

That Saturday morning I had the milk round completed for around 9.30 am. I managed a shower and a quick breakfast, and at about 10.30 started to make my way down Lock Hill to the Kwik Save car park. I arrived around 10.45 am and many protesters were already there with banners and placards – the usual faces. I noticed Brian and Margaret

Ashmore. They were there with their son Jonathan and his wife Carmen; although I never remembered them at the beginning of the campaign, they were now keen protesters and were always with us. Carol Dye, Ann Nettleship with sister June, Alistair, Steve Birch, Becky Fryer, Steve Martin with his wife Sue and their children, Ann and Trevor Cockerill were the others I picked out. Now the numbers were growing as the time headed towards 11.00 am.

Then we heard them coming, singing SARP songs; someone had a drum. The protesters from Beighton had arrived, led by David Milsom and Avril Gold, around 100 or so had walked the three or four miles to our village. We joined with the Beighton protesters and moved off down Sheffield Road, led by the Grim Reaper. As we passed the fancy dress shop on the left, I wondered how long it would be before I took the one who led us home.

We passed the Angel just before the junction with Ellisons Road at 10.55, and there, coming down to pass the entrance to the Rother Valley Country Park we caught the first glimpse of the 150 or so Kiveton and Wales Bar protesters. We waited for them and we all marched on to SARP UK together, now about 600 to 700 protesters strong. It did not matter what Inspector Dick Severns said, tankers would be held up; this was a lot of protesters and there was no way that any vehicles would get through. We put Steve

Martin's flat-back lorry across the gates to be used as a platform, and we had a loudspeaker system installed.

Alan Charles was first to speak. "I want to say what a great turnout, you have let SARP UK know that you are not going away. I have had great concerns about this plant and all the recent errors – the rocket fuel, the dangers we are all in – we cannot let up our campaign, we must stay strong and we will finally close this place."

Ann Nettleship took the mike and made a great speech about the RASP campaign, what we all hoped to achieve and the reason she and her sister June stood at the gates of SARP with the Toxic Night Shift night after night. They would not stop until the incinerator was shut and the other processes were closed.

Owd Tup, aka Dave Froggatt, made a rare appearance at one of our protests. Dave was well in his seventies with a full head of grey hair and a weatherbeaten face; he seemed to walk everywhere, no South Yorkshire Transport for Dave, always Shanks's pony. Dave spoke of how he lived closer to the plant than almost anyone, down Primrose Lane, and how been witness to years of pollution, especially through the night as first Leigh and now SARP UK had poisoned us with their toxic emissions.

The early light rain had now turned much heavier, and as we stood, collars upturned, Owd Tup read the latest poem he had put to paper.

I Have to Say

I have to say to those who feel the fears I voice are just not real
Consider all the past mistakes and think again for all sakes
I have to say to all those whom decry these prophesies of doom
These prophesies are meant to be a warning 'gainst complacency.
I have to say, those orange skies have made the world realise
The dangers that we all are faced, when far too near these sites are placed
I have to say, each night I pray that soon our fears are swept away
At last we'll learn that SARP are leaving, before, I trust, we've cause for grieving.
I have to say my wish so dear, let children grow up free from fear.
Not have to face life 'neath a cloud and know too soon the Reaper's shroud.
I have to say a thousand things, of what I fear the future brings.
How soon or late the Reaper's call, will drape us 'neath our funeral pall
I have to say, re: SARP UK, I hope that ne'er will come the day
When, midst the carnage, grief and woe,
I have to say I told you so.

To rapturous applause, Dave Froggatt placed the mike back on its stand, turned, and dropped from the back of the wagon in a way that belied his years.

I was the last to speak. "I repeat the words spoken earlier, a fantastic turnout, SARP UK know we are all in this for the long haul and our commitment is as strong as ever. Talking of commitment, that is a word I would not use for the Derbyshire County Council Education Committee, headmasters at the Sheffield Road and Eckington schools. They and the governors have been nonexistent in their support of our fight against this company. They have not helped in the case of the Sheffield Road schools but they have done their best to obstruct our fight. The teachers in these schools… there is not one here today, but there must be many amongst them know what we fight for today is more important than their next wage packet. I hope they lie easy with their conscience when this is all over and we have won. The children may one day ask them, 'What did you do, Miss, in the fight against SARP UK?'"

The green and white tankers stood bumper to bumper all the way back to the end of Ellisons Road. The police were helpless, they could not move the best part of 700 protesters who didn't want to be moved, they were well undermanned. The few police who were there were resigned to the fact that until reinforcements arrived or the protest was over nobody was going anywhere. There were many of the police there, although they could never admit it, backing us 100 percent, like the six officers from nearby Bolsover. They all knew all about dioxins – they had the infamous Coalite plant in their village. Coalite had been responsible for Agent Orange, used in the Vietnam War by the US military as a chemical herbicide and defoliant known as Rainbow Herbicides. It is estimated that two million Vietnamese suffered illnesses and half a million babies were born with birth defects as a result of Agent Orange. Coalite had been responsible for the nearby River Doe Lea becoming known as the most dioxin-polluted river in the world. Yes, those six officers from our neighbouring village of Bolsover were well aware of the dangers we all faced.

The meeting ended, the behaviour of the protesters defiant but well-mannered. Inspector Dick Severns of the Derbyshire Constabulary knew we were not members of some radical group, we were just ordinary people trying to close this poison plant the only way we knew how.

That Monday, *The Sheffield Star* headline was "Hundreds in SARP Protest." Tony Belshaw wrote: "Confrontation between campaigners and police at the SARP UK chemicals plant in Killamarsh failed to materialise at the latest rally. The stage had been set for ugly scenes after police threatened to arrest protesters who stopped tankers from carrying materials into the plant. Campaigners were adamant drivers would not pass. No deliveries were made when 700 protesters gathered outside the plant as three separate marches were held from Killamarsh, Beighton and Kiveton Park.

"John Moran for Residents Against SARP Pollution (RASP) told the rally, 'This place has poisoned us, put the safety of our children at risk.' He also slammed local headmasters for failing to support them in the campaign. The plant lies a quarter of a mile from Killamarsh Junior and Infant Schools."

Chapter Thirteen

Emissions Crackdown

September 17, 1998 was going to be a significant day in the fight to close SARP UK. The phone rang early that Thursday morning.

"Morning, John." The day was long gone when Alistair needed to identify himself. "The Environment Agency are to make an announcement concerning the incinerator, not sure what, but if I hear anything I will be back in touch. Speak with you later."

SARP were desperate to get the incinerator working; the site's profitability was greatly reduced whilst this was not in operation. We were equally determined to keep it shut down, as it had been since the two leaks last May. The only difference now with the past was that, with the help of our technical expert Ian Legge, we had become expert at knowing what emission levels were allowed on all SARP's processes, something prior to May we had only guessed at.

Since then, with Ian's help, we had certain members who had gone to Chesterfield Town Hall, where, as in every major town, incidents of illegal releases to the air have by law to be recorded on public records. We had found over the last two years SARP UK and Leigh Environmental had been responsible for some huge releases. The limits on sulphur dioxide from the incinerator had been 100 mg/m^3; we knew from the public records that in a particular emission, they had recorded 8,000 mg/m^3. Even a non-chemist like myself knew that was exceeding the limits by 80 times. The emission on another occasion was 5,500 mg/m^3 – that was 55 times the limit. There were many more recordings of illegal emissions and the EA appeared to have turned a blind eye; obviously SARP/Leigh had been very happy with self-regulation, they thought, and quite rightly, no one else seemed to check up. That was until we appeared on the scene.

In the event of SARP restarting the incinerator, we would be checking their releases and asking the EA to monitor them on a day-to-day basis. This time SARP – or the EA for that matter – dare not make any errors. We were watching them.

The silence of my study that Thursday morning was broken by the sound of my fax machine receiving a message.

PRESS RELEASE

From the Environment Agency, Templeborough, Rotherham

The Environment Agency have informed SARP UK at Killamarsh that releases from its chemical incinerator do not comply with the conditions of its license.

We have now issued an enforcement notice, ordering the company to meet limits on releases.

The Environment Agency had also slashed levels of chemicals the incinerator was allowed to give off. Sulphur dioxide releases had been halved to 50 mg/m^3 and the limit for hydrogen chloride had been cut from 100 mg/m^3.

I gave the following quote to the press: "We welcome the tightening up of the emissions, obviously, but we are not looking for the reopening of the incinerator, we are looking for the closure of the plant."

The papers also reported SARP UK's statement, which said that it continued to invest in and to develop the Killamarsh site. "The enforcement notice does not in any way change that commitment. There has been a chemical plant at Killamarsh for 150 years," the statement added. "SARP UK does not plan to relocate the facility, instead we plan to invest in the facility to improve operating standards and safety.

Through this process we can remain a local employer while addressing the issues which are currently causing a public concern."

I knew that because of our intense pressure and the revelations we had unearthed, the Environment Agency had been forced to take these steps. These illegal emissions had happened before the May incidents, for what other reason would the EA bring them up now, mid September, almost six months later?

At the Monday meeting at the Crown we reviewed RASP's financial position. Pat Whitehouse, our treasurer, gave us the following details. We had a total of £1300.33, taken through various collections at protests and round the village. We were looking quite healthy financially for a change.

Wendy Wellings, our Chair, asked Ian Legge if there had been any progress with the test kits that had been discussed at the last meeting. Our idea was that with these test kits we could take our own soil samples in and around Killamarsh. Ian said that he would give a demonstration after the meeting to the six members of his team and hoped they could return them to him by Sunday.

Wendy then turned to me and said, "John, what are your thoughts about the new enforcements on SARP regarding emissions?"

"I think last Thursday's announcement by the EA as regards emissions is one of our greatest victories. The question I have asked myself over and again since that announcement is, how can SARP keep to a limit of 10 mg/m^3 cubed when they couldn't keep to 100 mg/m^3, and how with the sulphur dioxide emissions can they keep to 50 mg/m^3 when they couldn't keep to 100 mg/m^3? The answer is they can't. Ian Legge advises me that £3 million would have to be spent on this incinerator to be able to burn to those levels. SARP are only talking of investing £350,000 on the site. I don't think that such a clapped-out site as SARP could ever expect such investment and the alternative is that if they reopen the incinerator we only have to wait and watch these limits, that I believe will prove impossible for them to keep to with their second-hand incinerator."

The next story we released to *The Sheffield Star* on September 22 ran like this:

"Picket Threat in SARP UK Row – Companies who do business with SARP UK Industrial Waste Plant at Killamarsh near Sheffield may be picketed by protesters as the campaign to close the plant intensifies. The group RASP plan to write to every business currently sending waste to the plant to ask them to use an alternative site; if they don't, the group plans to picket them. RASP is setting up its own air-quality monitoring equipment to check emissions from the SARP plant. RASP is also planning to have soil samples taken from land near to the site to see if pollution has entered the local environment."

The following night we had around 30 protesters at the gates. One of them – no one seemed to know him, which we thought strange – slipped through the SARP gates and apparently went for a walk around the site. The security staff failed to see him enter, and it was only an hour later a chemist on site there spotted him and, after challenging him and having no response, phoned the police. They arrived, went on to the site and came back with this guy in handcuffs. RASP used the story once again to our advantage, passing it on to *The Sheffield Star*. That Thursday's edition contained the headline, "Protester Arrested at SARP Waste Plant", and went on to describe the incident in more detail.

"Police arrested a protester found wandering around the controversial SARP UK waste plant at Killamarsh last night. The man slipped between chained gates and knocked on the window of an office containing security staff before embarking on a tour of the site. Staff eventually called police, the man was arrested and driven away to the applause of other protesters at the gates of the plant.

"'He was able to enter the plant and knock on a window at the security guards. He wasn't noticed so he went for a walk around the plant,' said John Moran of protest group RASP, which is calling for the closure of the site following many incidents at the site and pollution scares. 'This shows what alarming security there is at this site, that is just about the most dangerous waste plant in the UK.'

"Killamarsh Inspector Dick Severns said the unnamed man was interviewed and released without charge late last night."

The mystery would remain forever: who was he? Where did he come from?

The next day we staged an early-morning protest at the SARP gates. Someone had brought a big banner that they drooped over the gates, proclaiming in foot-high letters: SARP CLOSED TODAY. This too was run in *The Sheffield Star*, whose front page featured it as a half-page spread. It also showed a photo of someone carrying a big placard saying, "ROCKET REFUEL STATION FILL UP HERE".

Under the headline "We've Shut You Down – Chemical Plant 'Closed Today', Say Protesters," Steve Caddy wrote, "Protesters staged a surprise blockade outside the gates of controversial waste plant SARP UK. Around 40 protesters arrived at 7.15 am to stop tankers and staff from entering or leaving the Killamarsh plant at the centre of a closure campaign. Two police officers arrived and warned protesters to move away from the gates. But tankers were able to move forward a few feet before protesters again brought them to a halt. The confrontation ended in a half-hour stalemate until the arrival of Killamarsh Inspector Dick Severns. He warned the protesters to clear the road. 'I'm asking you to move because you are obstructing the highway. If you refuse to move you will be arrested. Even if you are walking around in front of the tankers you are still causing an obstruction,' he said. But the protesters held their ground until the police reinforcements arrived and then and only then did they stage a slow march along the full length of Ellisons Road followed by a queue of tankers and lorries."

That wet autumn day I walked slowly up the middle of Ellisons Road, so no one could pass. To my left walked Brian and Margaret Ashmore, Becky Fryer, Ann Nettleship and her sister June. The 250 yards took us ten minutes to cover. As the rain poured, in the morning gloom the lights reflected off the wet road from the green and white tankers that stretched back as far as you could see, with smaller white SARP vans trying to squeeze past. Every time they did, an elderly man with greying hair carrying a "SARP UK GET OUT" banner did a quick sidestep to his left; the man in the black beret with defiant eyes as always, strong as ever.

At the Monday meeting at the Crown someone gave me a photo they had taken as we walked that 250 yards. I was dressed in jeans and a blue windcheater, maroon shirt just visible and a black flat hat, beneath which was a face that looked as if it had no sleep for a long time, pale, drawn and gaunt. This was one picture that didn't lie. When this was over I would sleep for a year, I promised myself.

A few days later, I received an early morning telephone call from *The Socialist* paper, who were always interested in environmental issues. They did not want to speak with me; they had heard about and reported on our fight with SARP UK, but they wanted to do a piece about the Toxic Night Shift and speak to someone who could describe what a typical "shift" was like.

Sandra wrote the article. This was how it appeared in the newspaper under the headline, "On the Toxic Night Shift."

"Residents of Killamarsh have been protesting against SARP UK chemical plant since May, when a cloud of toxic gas surrounded the area. Sandra, a member of Residents Against SARP Pollution, tells *The Socialist* what it's like on the protest 'night shift.'

"'At about 10.30 pm myself and three protesters get ready to spend a night down at the gates of SARP UK Killamarsh. It's cold so we get lots of woolly jumpers on, fill our flasks and set off for the plant. We park at the entrance gates for about an hour, just to let the security guards know we've arrived and that they're not going to have a quiet night. Around 2.00 am we park our cars in the back roads so security don't know whether we've gone home or not. The buildings, trees and shrubbery leading down to the plant provide plenty of places to hide whilst still being able to get a good view of the entrance.

"'It is pretty quiet on a night now since the protesters have been going down. Before the two big incidents there were tankers going in and out all through the night. I suppose that why the chimney was churning out thick black smoke which choked us all between midnight and 5.00 am. About 2.30 am the security guards leave the plant to look for protesters. We know they're coming because they have to remove a large chain and padlock from the gates – they try to do it quietly but the sound carries in the still of the night. This is when we make ourselves invisible, lying flat and completely still. We can see the light from their torches going in out of the trees and bushes. They continue to the top of the road and come back.

"'When the guards are back on plant we have a good laugh and congratulate ourselves for being smarter than them. This is repeated again at about 3.15 am and again we are not spotted. At about 3.30 am the first tanker driver arrives. We carefully make our way down to the entrance, weaving in and out of trees. Once we hear the tankers start up we move towards the gates. We come out of our hiding places and run towards the entrance, spread ourselves across the road and completely block the gates. The security guards and tanker drivers get very frustrated and tell us to move away. They say they are "sick to death" of us and wish we would "piss off". We stand our ground. "We'll send for the police." shouts one of the guards, but we stand our ground. It can take 15 to 45 minutes for the police to arrive. Up to now, most officers have been quite friendly and sympathetic towards us. They ask us to stand aside and let the tankers out – we keep them talking just to delay the tankers for a bit longer. Eventually the police say "If you don't clear the highway we'll have to arrest you." With this we move aside and let the tankers out to the sound of jeers and "SARP OUT!" It's now about 5.00 am. We are all cold and wet, but we feel pleased with ourselves. We walk back to our cars, say goodnight and off home to bed. So SARP UK, you said we wouldn't be seen when it got cold and wet. How wrong you are.'"

After Sandra's article, the next piece of news to catch the eye of RASP appeared in Derbyshire County Council's monthly magazine. A headline boasted "Cash Boost for Awards Scheme" above a photo of Derbyshire County Council leader Martin Doughty receiving cheques from Doug Davis, General Manager of Onyx Environmental Trust, and Tom Spaul, Managing Director of Onyx UK.

The accompanying text read: "And the winner is Derbyshire environment. The Greenwatch scheme, including the popular annual awards for local groups dedicated to protecting and improving the environment, has received a special £40,000 bonus. The boost has come courtesy of Onyx Environmental Trust via direct contributions from Onyx Environmental Group and the landfill tax scheme. It means that this year's 10th anniversary awards will be bigger and better than before – with the County Council providing the lucky winners."

The fact that Derbyshire County Council and Martin Doughty were still taking "the money" was a constant source of aggravation to RASP. SARP poisoned us in Killamarsh, SARP bought the silence of the Derbyshire County Council and everyone under their umbrella. One day sometime in the future we would confront them, to let them know who is really "paying the price".

It was Monday September 28, 1998. The Crown meeting started a little after 7.30 pm. "I know we have a busy week ahead, so I will give the floor to Alistair."

"Thanks, Wendy, yes, we are planning to go to SARP's premises at Brownhills, near Walsall, on Wednesday. We know that they have had plenty of problems at this plant, they too were previously with Leigh Environmental and have a similar profile to SARP UK in Killamarsh. How many are there that are going to Brownhills?"

About 10 people put their hand up to go, including me.

"It will take us around two hours, we have to be down there for 12.00 midday, so we will meet at the Kwik Save car park and get away for 10.00 am."

Chapter Fourteen

Hijack at the Swallow

The following Wednesday morning I was up as usual at 3.00 am, picked my two helpers up and we managed to complete the round for just after 8.00 am. I returned home and, after a shower and breakfast, I rung my delivery order to the dairy for the following morning. That day, although I didn't know it yet, was going to be a long one.

Just after 10.00 am, three cars pulled away from the Kwik Save car park. I had in my car Carol Dye, Allison Sampson and Ann Cockerill. In the other car was Alistair, Brian and Margaret Ashmore and Steve Birch. The third car contained Tony Ward, Margaret Marsh and Becky Fryer. The weather was absolutely appalling, with very heavy rain, and the windows in the car were forever steaming up, but as we neared Walsall, the nearest place to Brownhills, the weather appeared to improve slightly. We made our way to the entrance of the site, but the actual office, unlike at Killamarsh, was a long way from the highway and the protest would not be as effective. Nevertheless, we all piled out at the terminal where the SARP tankers left and entered the site. Despite the rain, which had now returned to being heavy, we soon had tankers backing up on both sides of the gates.

Protesters at Brownhills had been many, but as at Killamarsh, after 1986 had faded away to face years of pollution at the hands of these criminals. On the day we arrived, whether the West Midlands Constabulary were understaffed, or whether it was because they didn't expect us, whatever the reason, we were left unhindered, and for a long time no tanker – and there were many – moved in or out. Finally the West Midlands police force arrived, in three police cars and a riot van. We took our time responding, affecting not to understand the Walsall accent. The police officer warned us that if it happened again there would be arrests. He had obviously not been in touch with the Derbyshire Constabulary for our profile. An hour later, the same police officer was back to clear the next backlog that had accumulated. By this time it was around 2.30 pm, and at that moment my mobile started to ring. It was Graham Readfearn from the news desk of *The Yorkshire Post*.

"John, SARP UK have just issued a press release that they are to hold a press conference tonight at the Swallow

Hotel in Sheffield. They have only announced it in the last few minutes, and it is due to start around 5.30 pm; I thought you would want to know."

The Swallow Hotel was definitely an expensive place, situated in the Nether Edge area of Sheffield. I was dressed in an old Barbour jacket and jeans, OK for delivering milk in bad weather, not exactly what one expects at the Swallow Hotel. The rest of the Brownhills party looked only marginally better. We alerted the rest of RASP and they planned to converge on the meeting in time for the 5.30 pm start.

Having made our way as quickly as possible through the easing rain and mist back from the Midlands, we arrived in the car park of the hotel at around 5.15. We made our way to the front door, where a big guy blocked our way. "You cannot come in here, sir, this is a private meeting. Only invited guests and press."

With that, Alistair, who had expected this, opened his rain-soaked jacket to reveal an expensive camera round his neck. "Press," he declared, and ducking under the man's outstretched arm, he walked straight on and up the stairs, following "SARP Press Conference" signs. The big guy's resistance collapsed at this point, and so the rest of the group simply followed the now disappearing Alistair as he entered the room at the top of the stairs. We found ourselves in a large meeting room. The press conference had just started; Philippe

Girard MD for SARP UK was just about to speak from the top table. Alistair, who was just in front of us, went into full flow, ably backed up by Steve Birch at all of five feet five inches, some way below Alistair, but determined to be heard.

Alistair directed his attack at Philippe Girard. "Why won't you talk to the people you are affecting? You, Girard, you won't come and face us. Why is it you'll never talk to the actual members of the community affected by the actions of your company?" With this Philippe Girard and all the SARP men fled the room, leaving an empty top table, a row of TV cameras and press reporters, stunned by the quick exit of the Frenchman and his top aides. RASP, never at a loss for words, decided that as SARP had vacated the press conference, we would not waste this opportunity and we would hold our own in its place.

I saw Carol Dye turning the names on the card holders around and writing three new names: John Moran, Alan Charles and Alistair Tice. Sitting in the oldest, scruffiest milk coat with shirt to match, drying out slightly from the drowning we had suffered at Brownhills, I leaned towards the mike. "John Moran, Press Officer, RASP, questions please."

For the next 30 minutes we answered questions from the media. The other members of RASP enjoyed SARP's hospitality by clearing plates of smoked salmon, pork pies and sandwiches kindly left by the fleeing French.

The events were widely reported in the media next day. Graham Readfearn's article for *The Yorkshire Post* proclaimed "Protesters Hijack Waste Plant Meeting". His article read: "Protesters campaigning to rid their village of an industrial waste plant hijacked a press conference called by the firm yesterday, overshadowing news that operations at the plant were to be scaled down. SARP UK directors abandoned their conference before a word was spoken after more than 20 uninvited people stormed into the room to unleash a tirade of criticism and demand the firm close the plant at Killamarsh near Sheffield.

"SARP UK, which is at the centre of investigations into a string of leaks and mishaps, was about to announce plans to close three of its five operations at the site. But the protest group RASP (Residents Against SARP Pollution) filled the space left by the directors and held its own press conference after the company Managing Director, Philippe Girard, refused to speak to them.

"RASP member Alistair Tice asked directors, 'Why won't you talk to the people you're affecting? Philippe Girard won't come and face us. Why is it you'll never talk to the actual members of the community affected by the actions of your company?'

"Killamarsh resident Margaret Marsh, who also got into the press conference, said, 'Their children don't go to a school 150 metres from a chemical plant that isn't up to safety standards.'

"RASP spokesman John Moran, joined at the impromptu protesters' press conference by Mr. Tice and Derbyshire County Council member Alan Charles, said, 'We won't do any deal with SARP UK. We've had 20 years of pollution and fear. The end has come. SARP has to go.'

"Coun. Charles criticised SARP for not inviting the villagers, and said the company had already cancelled a liaison committee meeting scheduled for tonight without reason. SARP UK had organised the press conference at the Swallow Hotel in Sheffield yesterday afternoon to reveal plans to move its acid plant, oil plant and transport depot elsewhere. The firm has appointed Sheffield University's Environmental Consultancy (ECUS) to do a full inspection of the site in an attempt to take it above current national and European standards.

"But RASP members were adamant that their campaign would not stop until the plant had closed down completely. Mr. Moran, a local milkman, said bluntly, 'We're here to tell this company we don't want them in Killamarsh – we don't trust them.'"

The press conference came to a close, the reporters still scribbling notes from their new and unexpected sources. I was just about to join the other members of RASP in devouring the last of the smoked salmon and beef sandwiches, when a young man in his thirties approached. "Tom Ingle of the BBC, John, they would like you to do an interview at BBC Radio Sheffield. I have a car waiting."

I left the Swallow Hotel and soon Tom was weaving his way through the rush-hour traffic across Eccleshall Road towards the studios. As he drove he told me, "When you have finished your interview with us, ITV would like you to go to their Sheffield studios in Charter Square to do a live debate with Philippe Girard, about whether SARP UK should stay or go."

The radio interview over, Tom showed me back down through the foyer to my waiting taxi.

The white taxi's engine was ticking over as I slid into the back seat. Turning to me, the driver said, "Change of plans, Mr. Moran, we now have to go to Kirkstall Road, Leeds, ITV's main studio in Yorkshire."

Philippe Girard, MD for SARP UK, senior executive of the Vivendi Corporation, employer of 350,000 people worldwide, had said, "I won't talk to the milkman." That was how *The Sheffield Star* reported the event the following day. Philippe Girard had told ITV, "I do not want to share a studio, and wish it to be done by live relay." Hence my 80-mile round trip to Leeds.

While I was en route and preparing to go on air, M. Girard, protected from having to talk to the milkman, was being interviewed by Christa Ackroyd. He told her, "We've taken action to ensure the Killamarsh site is in future fully capable of exceeding statutory standards. The enquiry is fully independent of SARP, and ECUS will decide its own scope and direction. I have guaranteed ECUS full access to the Killamarsh site and my management team." M. Girard said the move was intended as an act of "good faith" towards the community. But he admitted that when the company took over the site from Leigh Environmental last January, the conditions were "worse than expected". "As we have said from the beginning, we are truly sorry for any anxiety which people in the community have suffered," he said. "This was, to say the least, an unfortunate legacy. We have considered taking legal action in relation to our purchase, but we have been advised that we would be unlikely to succeed."

Christa Ackroyd also did the Calendar News interview with me for ITV, Philippe Girard having already been able to give his side unopposed from his "safe" studio in Sheffield. She started by saying, "There can be nobody in our region that has not heard of the environmental protest group RASP, or Residents Against SARP Pollution, from the village of Killamarsh in North East Derbyshire. I have with me tonight John Moran, who combines his early morning job of village milkman with being Press Officer for RASP. Mr. Phillipe Girard, MD for SARP Industries, is in our studio and says that they intend to restart the incinerator soon in Killamarsh, and they intend to spend at least £1 million to bring it up to standard. What is RASP's response to that, because we all know that RASP have long opposed the reopening of this process?"

"RASP's response to that is simple. We know that the SARP UK plant at Killamarsh is on its last legs, it is a dangerous, decaying plant. We know what SARP UK will spend and it is not £1 million – they are trying to wriggle out of paying for new oil scrubbers, and the cost of that would only be a fraction of £1 million. SARP UK might be a lot of things, but they are not stupid – they know as well as RASP that to get this plant up to standard it would cost the best part of three to four million. But at Killamarsh everything is on the cheap, that is why it is so dangerous. RASP warns SARP UK here tonight, you start your incinerator and we will be watching, we now have our own air pollution monitors and if you exceed any emissions we will know. We are watching you 24 hours a day and have made the Environment Agency do their job, no more coming on 24 hours after a member of the community has made a complaint, no more tea and biscuits in the manager's office. They are now being made to police this site like they should have done these last 20 years."

Christa then said, "Mr. Philippe Girard says that he is closing certain processes at the plant: acid, oil and transport are to be scaled down to make the running of the site more simple. How do you respond to that?"

"RASP welcomes the permanent closure of these three processes," I replied.

"What is RASP's response to Mr. Girard's claim that RASP has caused people to lose their jobs; they are now making 50 people redundant at the SARP plant?"

I answered, "We all know about job losses in Killamarsh, we are an old mining village. Hundreds lost their jobs with the closing of the High Moor and Westthorpe collieries, but every job has a price, and in the case of SARP UK that is a price too high."

The interview ended with Christa Ackroyd saying, "RASP has staged protest after protest: will you continue with these in the future?" to which I replied, "We will continue with the protests, we will continue to disrupt this company whenever we can."

The lights dimmed and it was over. The taxi dropped me outside my house on the corner of Belklane Drive at 8.30 pm that night. I had been on the go since 3.00 am, it had been a long day.

Chapter Fifteen

The Dawn Rooftop Protest

The next morning, Thursday October 1, was the day we planned to have the rooftop protest. I made my way down Ellisons Road at just after 6.30 am. As I neared the gates there were about 40 protesters already outside, and there on the roof were Alastair and Louise Wellings. The dawn was just breaking. Alistair was stood up about 12 feet from Louise, who was crouched on the end of the roof's apex. Alistair was holding a white "SARP UK Out" banner and Louise a little wooden cross bearing the words "SARP UK GO GO GO".

The police were soon on the scene; they rushed through the gates but there was no way that they were going to get them down. The media were there in force, BBC and ITV Yorkshire cameras whirring, they caught the two protesters against the breaking early morning sun, Alistair in a red top and Louise with her face half covered by a scarf and a waterproof jacket with the hood up. We all knew how terrified of heights Louise was, and as she sat on the apex of the roof many feet off the ground, we all had our hearts in our mouths, her mum Wendy most of all.

By 7.45 am the crowd of protesters at the gates had grown to maybe 100 people as the news had spread about the rooftop protest. Workers from all the other different businesses based on the Norwood Industrial Estate had also started to gather to watch the drama unfold. The place was in chaos; the original 30 protesters had blocked the roads and tankers were backing up everywhere inside the plant and down Ellisons Road, workers could not get in or out. Other transport companies, notably Amtrak, could not reach their depot because of the traffic jams. Eventually at 9.00 Alistair and Louise came down, to be arrested by the waiting police.

Later that day Steve Caddy wrote about the protest in *The Sheffield Star*, under the headline, "Rooftop Mum Arrested; Police Hold Two After Dawn Gas Plant Protest." The article went on to say, "Angry protesters were arrested today after staging a dramatic rooftop protest at the controversial SARP UK waste recycling plant. Two members of the RASP campaign group had entered the Killamarsh plant through an unlocked gate and used a ladder to climb on to the roof. Alistair Tice and mother of two Louise Wellings were cheered on by campaigners, who then blocked the main gate to prevent tankers leaving and entering the site until the police arrived. After an hour and a half, the police said they would try to talk the two into coming down.

"'We are not going to send anyone up on the roof. I don't want to put my officers or the protesters at risk,' said Inspector Robert King. 'However, they will be arrested for aggravated trespass.' But after two hours the protesters gave up their rooftop vigil of their own accord.

"RASP spokesman John Moran pledged that the surprise protests would continue until the plant was closed. 'We will keep disrupting this firm. We will vary our tactics so they don't know what we are going to do next.' The group regretted any possible redundancies caused by the scaling-down operations, which follows an announcement by SARP yesterday. 'We don't want anyone to lose their jobs, this firm is big enough to relocate anyone who wants to keep working for them,' said Mr. Moran. 'Any job losses will be regrettable but we have got to think of the future health of our children for years to come.'

"The company has announced that it is ending operations at the site's acid plant, oil plant and transport depot, affecting up to 50 jobs. Talks are taking place with staff over possible transfers. SARP has also appointed Sheffield University Environmental Consultancy (ECUS) to carry out full and independent audit of the plant with the aim of improving it to exceed all current safety standards. John Moran, RASP spokesman, said, 'We are suspicious of ECUS, their wages are being paid by SARP UK. How can that be independent? They cannot change the condition of this toxic plant, this plant is falling apart, the tanks are rupturing, the toxic barrels are leaking. The sooner all processes are closed the better.'

"In a press interview after being released from police custody 12 hours later, Louise Wellings said, 'I did the protest for the future of my children, Richard aged 10 and Nicholas aged seven, who don't have a voice according to SARP. I climbed the rooftop to protest peacefully and visibly so everyone would know how we all feel, just a stone's throw from that stinking plant.'"

The courageous Louise Wellings (right of photo) and Alistair Tice on the roof of SARP UK's administrative building in Killamarsh. Their dramatic protest would see them end up in court.

Alistair and Louise were released but with strict bail conditions. In Alistair's case he was banned from entering Killamarsh and in the case of Louise she was banned from going within 500 yards of SARP's premises. As her house was probably not that distance from SARP's gate they looked very harsh conditions to keep. They would appeal.

The case was due to go before Chesterfield Magistrates' Court on November 19, at the same time as the Health and Safety Executive's prosecution of SARP UK.

A few days later, Monday October 4, another article by Steve Caddy in *The Sheffield Star* gave more details about the escalating legal action against SARP. Headlined "Chemical Leak Row Firm Is Prosecuted", the article read: "Waste recycling firm SARP UK is to be prosecuted by environment watchdogs for a pollution scare at its controversial Killamarsh plant. The Environment Agency announced today that it will be prosecuting the company following the chemical leak on May 14. It follows a decision by the Health and Safety Executive to prosecute the company for the same leak. Both prosecutions follow an investigation by both bodies into the incident and a second leak on May 30. Any legal action over the second leak will be decided later this month. SARP UK faces two charges by the Environment Agency: that on May 14 it treated controlled special waste – sulphuric and nitric acid – in a manner likely to cause pollution of the environment or harm to human health, contrary to the

Environmental Protection act 1990; that on May 14 it kept the controlled special waste in a manner likely to cause pollution of the environment or harm to human health, contrary to the Environment Protection Act.

"As in the Health and Safety action, the firm faces a fine of £20,000 for each offence if the case is dealt with by magistrates, or an unlimited fine if it goes to Crown Court."

Tuesday October 6, 1998 started as usual. I was up at 3.00 am – the mornings were dark now, unlike earlier in the campaign, the long summer days just a memory now the colder, wetter autumn days were here. We finished the round just after 8.00 am and then after a quick breakfast and shower I was ready to go to Chesterfield with about 30 RASP members to witness what the magistrates were going to do about the strict bail conditions imposed by the police against, as they were now known, "The Rooftop Two".

We all stood on the lawn outside the courts in Chesterfield, a new building near to the town hall. We had our placards and banners, the media was there as usual. We all trooped into the courtroom: Ann Cockerill, Roger Barraclough, Allison Sampson, my wife Sandra, Becky Fryer, Bev Smith, Brian and Margaret Ashmore and Terry and May Hobson. There was only room for about a dozen, so the others waited outside. Alistair and Louise sat up at the front table with their solicitor Danny Simpson and we all waited for the three magistrates to appear. Once they had arrived, the chief magistrate sitting in the middle, John Friel, rose to his feet and said, "Today I have to consider the bail conditions that the police have imposed on the people before me, namely Alistair Tice and Louise Wellings. The police argue that their behaviour in staging a rooftop protest at the premises of SARP UK was a case of going too far. I have considered these bail conditions most carefully. I realise that the RASP protesters have been in a long-running campaign to close this toxic waste plant, but what they did overstepped the recognised mark of peaceful protesting, in that they trespassed unlawfully on SARP UK's premises. With all that in mind, I feel that the police have also 'gone too far' and the right to protest is important." He added that protests had to be kept within the law, but at this point we were all on our feet cheering Mr. Friel's decision. He was most annoyed and told us all, "I wish to remind you all that this is not a circus but a court of law and at any further outburst I will clear my court."

We all returned to our seats, and although said in a soft voice, Carol Dye's "A bit of a grumpy old sod, isn't he?" could be clearly heard. Mr. Friel continued, "I am going to lift the bans but impose a new condition, that Alistair and Louise promise not to enter the premises of SARP UK." They both nodded. "The new condition is that you do not obstruct tankers entering or leaving the site." They both nodded once again, and the case was adjourned till November 3.

We left the court. Louise and Alistair posed for press and television with all the 30 or so RASP members in the background with a banner declaring:

LOUISE & ALISTAIR
THEY DID IT FOR OUR CHILDREN
LET JUSTICE PREVAIL

The reporters gathered round me. "How does RASP feel about the court's decision, Mr. Moran?"

"We are delighted by the magistrate's decision, he has protected our right to protest and we feel that we have won another battle, but these conditions only apply to Alistair and Louise. The protests will continue and the tankers will be stopped."

They then turned to solicitor Danny Simpson. "Will your clients plead guilty on November 3, Mr. Simpson?"

"No, they intend to deny the charges on the grounds that their actions were not unlawful and the company's activities are."

The following morning 40 protesters gathered at the SARP UK gates. They were all wearing masks printed with the faces of Alistair and Louise to hide their identities. Tankers were held up for an hour, and again workers were unable to leave or enter, with other industrial estate transport thrown into chaos. The police arrived to find Tices and Wellingses everywhere.

The headline in *The Sheffield Star*, who reported the protest in full, was: "Guess Who?" with pictures of the masked protesters all with an eerie resemblance to the "Rooftop Two".

Monday October 19, 1998 was a momentous occasion – Philippe Girard had finally decided that after all these months he would meet the people of Killamarsh, and had agreed to attend a public meeting at the Village Centre.

Sandra and myself arrived a little after 7.20 pm, some 40 minutes before the 8.00 pm start to ensure we got a decent seat. The hall filled quickly and by 7.50 there was standing room only. At 7.55 pm Philippe Girard arrived, accompanied by his minders and a police escort. We had had to chase him round a Paris boardroom and a posh Sheffield hotel to get him here at Killamarsh that night.

On the platform there was, from the left, Laurie Edson, SARP's Technical Manager, who had previously worked for Leigh as a director with them since the early 1980s before joining SARP UK after the takeover in January, Philippe

Girard MD of SARP UK Industries, Alan Charles and Mary Dee of ECUS. Alan Charles chaired the meeting. He introduced Laurie Edson, who said, "We have brought in ECUS, the Sheffield University environmental team, who are experts and independent. We will abide by whatever their findings are."

Ann Nettleship was on her feet. "Who is paying for ECUS?"

Edson was speechless, but after recovering slightly he responded, "I don't think that is relevant."

"Well, we do, answer the question." Ann was not letting him off the hook.

"SARP UK have commissioned ECUS to do the report."

"So are you saying that SARP UK are paying them?"

"Yes, that is correct," was Edson's reluctant reply.

"Well, how can that be independent?" Ann had made her point. We all knew that although ECUS were a respected body, SARP UK, having paid them a huge fee, were now hiding behind a cloak of respectability that they hoped would reduce the flak they were getting from RASP. The new manager was Phil Howard, who together with Phil Rostance in PR were both old Leigh men going back to the 70s and 80s. They were battle-hardened, having been through so much with Leigh – you only had to ask the residents of

Walsall. They had been drafted in by SARP UK and we knew that they would not be as easy to deal with as some of the previous younger management.

The meeting continued. Mary Dee from ECUS said very little, only confirming they had been commissioned by SARP UK to do this report.

Alistair was the next to take aim. "Will ECUS be doing their own testing, or conducting community health risk assessments? Finally, if your report reaches the same conclusion as the RASP report, which is that the place should be closed, would you recommend the closure of this plant?"

"It's not my job to close the plant," retorted the ECUS boss.

Alistair responded, "Exactly. Your job is to whitewash SARP so they can reopen the incinerator plant, but we won't let them." He continued, "RASP members' own report, named 'SARP – A Suitable Case for Treatment', exposed the real carryings-on at this plant. Rocket fuel, arsenic, antimony and many more have been wrongly stored or illegally emitted this year alone. This report has been sent to Harry Barnes and he will comment on it in the Commons this week. You lot down at SARP have also been sent the same report."

Philippe Girard now spoke up, saying, "I would be happy to live in Killamarsh." This was greeted by cries from the audience, some unrepeatable. He continued by saying,

"There would always be a risk but it could be tackled by reducing it to its minimum level."

With this Terry Turner jumped to his feet. "What guarantees can you give us that these explosions and leaks that we have had this last 20 years won't happen again?"

To this Girard replied, "You can never guarantee there won't be another incident."

"Exactly, that is just the point that we are trying to make – it doesn't matter what ECUS say, it doesn't matter what you at SARP UK say, the danger will always be there whilst you are there."

Girard, now clearly losing the plot, said, "We now have this company and site under control."

"That's only because we have shut down six of your seven processes that you operated there," responded Sandra, now on her feet as well.

"As I was saying," continued Girard, "we now have things under control."

With that I was on my feet too; as I was on the front row I could turn to the audience as well as the platform. Holding a newspaper that had been given to me by a complete stranger on entering the hall, I held it so all could see. "Control, what control? This is today's *Nottingham Evening News*, midday edition, headline 'Miracle Escape from Lorry Crush'." I read on. "A motorist was pulled to safety seconds before a 16-tonne waste lorry flattened his car. The man was dragged to safety by his quick-thinking passenger before the lorry came smashing down on the parked VW Polo. She threw open her door and pulled the driver across the seats, he was halfway clear when the lorry trapped his legs. The accident happened at 6.25 am after the Leigh SARP Environmental truck went out of control outside Nottingham Crown Court." Turning to Girard, I said again, "Control, what control? Even your 16-tonne waste wagons are out of control, everything about you and SARP UK are. I have only one thing left to say – SARP UK, OUT, OUT OF KILLAMARSH!" With that the meeting broke up into chaos.

We made our way back home about 9.30 pm. As we neared my house we were greeted by the sight of it surrounded by police cars and a fire engine, flashing blue lights illuminating the scene. The following night's *Sheffield Star* told the story.

Under the headline, "Firebugs Target Van", the article said: "Police are investigating an attempted arson attack on a van owned by a prominent SARP chemical plant campaigner. Residents Against SARP Pollution spokesman John Moran said the attacker was disturbed as he poured petrol over a van he uses to deliver milk. Mr. Moran was at the public meeting in Killamarsh when the van was attacked outside his Killamarsh home. 'He had poured a load of petrol over the bonnet and was fumbling for his matches when my daughter

Faye disturbed him,' said Mr. Moran. 'It was pure luck that she opened the door to let the dogs out, they ran straight down the garden and started barking. He ran off, leaving the petrol can.' A Derbyshire police spokesman said that investigations were continuing."

CHAPTER SIXTEEN

Houses of Parliament

On October 21, 1998, SARP UK was the subject of a debate in the House of Commons in Westminster, London. Like all debates, the proceedings were recorded in the Hansard archives. This is an abridged version of what was said that day:

> Mr. Harry Barnes (North East Derbyshire): There have been two major incidents of clouds of acid vapour escaping from SARP UK Ltd at Killamarsh in my constituency. They presented considerable and serious dangers to the residents of Killamarsh and the surrounding areas, including parts of the constituencies of my hon. Friends the member for Rother Valley (Mr. Barron) and for Sheffield Attercliffe (Mr. Betts). The plant is situated close to housing and within a few hundred yards of a junior school. It is also on the borders of

the Rother Valley Country Park – I see my hon. Friend the Member for the Rother Valley in the chamber – which is used by thousands of people.

The reaction of the communities in Killamarsh and surrounding areas was dramatic. Everyone had had enough, and demanded the removal of the plant to a site away from areas of population.

A residents' committee was formed known as RASP – an anagram of SARP that stands for Residents Against SARP Pollution. It has persistently campaigned for the closure of the plant in dramatic style, including a visit to SARP's parent company Vivendi in Paris – a multinational that is embarrassed because it likes to portray itself as environmentally friendly.

Astonishingly, although SARP has been under constant supervision by the Killamarsh community since the second incident, it has failed to get its act together. A catalogue of incidents has been unearthed. On the day of my right hon. Friend's [Michael Meacher, Minister for the Environment] visit to Killamarsh, it was discovered that barrels of rocket fuel were stored close to the local junior school. My right hon. Friend will remember his visit to the school playing field, with the SARP plant site starkly nearby. The consignment of rocket fuel came in 1507 drums in 20 deliveries between 1993 and 1995. Of those, 184 were left to deteriorate and had to be stored under water. Some of the remaining drums were incinerated, while others remain in storage on the site. I know that my right hon. Friend is concerned about the matter, which is under investigation by the Environment Agency, as are five other incidents.

First, waste left on the ground, with serious smells affecting the community, when an old storage tank was being cleaned out. Secondly, substantial off-site odours were caused following leachate recycling. Thirdly, 20 tonnes of slurry were dumped on a landfill site. There are questions as to how that met the provisions of the waste disposal licence. Fourthly, the recirculation of effluent in storage tanks caused serious smells. Fifthly, a gas scrubber was not properly maintained, leading to a further inability to remove smells from waste.

There have been numerous other incidents, such as the sample bottles of aniline carried from Killamarsh to Teeside by TNT that leaked en route. The material is hazardous, and causes skin and eye irritation. TNT was not informed of the contents of the bottles. Past carbon monoxide releases from the incinerator have also been found not to have complied with the licence. Then a tanker started to leave the site, although a worker was still on top of it.

A series of reports is being prepared about SARP's operation at Killamarsh. The Health and Safety Executive and the Environment Agency are conducting three reports plus six other investigations, which I have described. SARP commissioned a report by W.S. Atkins after the first incident, it has not seen the light of day. The company is going on to commission a unit at Sheffield University to produce a further report, and the area's Member of the European parliament is undertaking his own enquiry. RASP has been first off the blocks and has published a report. In fact SARP has responded to it – it was published yesterday – in a four-page fax to me. That response is somewhat more speedy than the emergence of the reports commissioned.

The Minister for the Environment (Mr. Michael Meacher): I am very pleased that my hon. Friend the Member for North East Derbyshire (Mr. Barnes) has secured a debate on this most important subject. I pay him a very great tribute for the extremely thorough and persistent manner in which he has pursued this serious case – not least because, as he said, in the middle of the events he was struck down by illness. I know that I speak for everyone present when I say that we are delighted to see him fully active, in pursuit of these matters with all his accustomed vigour.

I should express my real and unreserved sympathy and concern for the Killamarsh residents' worry and anger about the two occurrences that my hon. Friend has described. As he said, I have taken the opportunity to visit the plant in order to see for myself at first hand what has led to the concerns. I want to put on record how tremendously impressed I was by the poignant and forceful manner in which members of Residents Against SARP Pollution presented their case. It made a very big impression on me.

With all the heightened activity due to the legal actions and the attention from government ministers, we at RASP were as busy as ever, with our fight feeling like it was at a tipping point.

The minutes of our meeting at the Crown on October 26 illustrated just how much we had going on. The minutes of the previous meeting were read, with a correction to the venue for Halloween – this to be held at the Crown at Killamarsh. Kevin was then tasked with chasing up the results of our soil samples.

There was a report from a meeting of RASP with two representatives from ECUS, John Tilney and Chris Routh, at which Ian Legge had presented a list of questions. ECUS apparently now wished to meet with the Parish Council, and would press SARP to restart the liaison meetings. They agreed to meet Dr. Dick van Steenis, the UK's leading expert on the effects of toxic emissions from chemical waste plants and landfill, who had been advising and helping RASP through his connection to Ken Coates MEP's Mansfield office. Ian Legge felt there was every chance of a fair report by ECUS, and having questioned them about the November deadline for their report, was told that this could be a first report to be followed by further reports. We had pushed ECUS to take in ground contamination but they would not do so; their report would be based on information provided by SARP. They will include a toxicologist on their team if needed and will be prepared to release interim reports to RASP.

Regarding the document we presented to Mr. Girard at the public meeting, SARP had responded in a letter to MP Harry Barnes, trying to rubbish the report and saying a lot of it refers to years past. They didn't make any mention of the reports that spoke of the current six ongoing investigations that Harry Barnes referred to in the House of Commons.

We also addressed the fact that Phil Howard was thought to be the new site manager at SARP UK. Since we believed him to be an old Leigh man, this would be an interesting appointment as SARP had told their new PR company to put clear blue water between new management and Leigh. We intended to try and prove the connection and show that the past was still with us. The next day, on checking the files left in the Sainsbury's carrier bag, sure enough we uncovered a letter dated 1984 addressed to Phil Howard at Leigh Environmental, Killamarsh.

After the arson attack on my van, SARP had been contacted to give a joint press statement with RASP, distancing SARP and RASP from such action. It took SARP UK four hours to respond, and in the end RASP went to press alone.

Harry Barnes was to contact schools for statistics of children using inhalers. RASP had already done this with no results, so perhaps a letter from our MP might put pressure on them to respond. Along similar lines, a survey was to be undertaken to record asthma and bronchial problems in the village.

At the meeting of our subgroup a list of 17 technical questions was prepared. We agreed to contact ECUS to ask them to making reducing pollution from the incinerator a part of their brief. Finally we agreed the week's protest schedule: Friday from 6.00 pm onwards outside SARP and the court appearance at Chesterfield on Tuesday at 9.30 am.

Lots of RASP supporters accompanied Louise Wellings and Alistair Tice to Chesterfield Court House on November 3 for their case over their rooftop protest arrest of October 1.

Alistair later recalled, "We were a bit nervous because we faced serious charges."

The charge sheet declared that on Thursday October 1 they had trespassed on the premises of SARP UK at Ellisons Road, Killamarsh, and disrupted a lawful activity, namely storage processing and haulage of chemicals and waste which persons engaged in on that land, contrary to Section 68 (1) and (3) of the Criminal Justice and Public Order Act 1994.

But we were also expectant because the court had been booked for three days and RASP hoped that our defence would publicly expose SARP's unlawful practices over the years. We wanted to turn the tables and put SARP UK in the dock.

Shortly after the case opened, our solicitor Danny Simpson, of Howells Solicitors in Sheffield, interrupted proceedings to ask the court to drop the charges on the grounds that SARP UK were not carrying out lawful business on that site.

Unbeknown to us, Danny had done his own inspection on the SARP site and taken photographs of the multiple holes in their perimeter fence, which should be inspected and maintained daily. He produced these photos for the court and asked for the charges to be dropped.

The prosecution barrister, who had come up from London with a plum in his mouth and didn't have a clue, once, twice, three times asked the magistrate for leave to consult his client and take instructions. The magistrate grew increasingly irritated by this and on the third occasion warned "Plummy" that this would be the last time.

Plummy came back into the court with his tail between his legs and confessed, "I don't think we have got a case."

There was jubilation. The charges were dropped, the Rooftop Two given conditional discharges on the promise they would not trespass on the site again, which was no problem as plenty of others in the RASP group were prepared to do that if necessary. Later, we felt a little cheated that SARP were not exposed to all three days for all their malpractices of the past.

However, it was a great relief for Louise and Alistair to be cleared and another victory for RASP in the fight against SARP. So with that we all went back to the Crown to celebrate.

Back in the Crown for our regular meeting the following Monday, Wendy Wellings opened the meeting as usual, sister Eileen by her side. Eileen I had known years before I came to Killamarsh in 1979, as she had been a customer of mine when I worked for Express Dairy in Sheffield. She now lived in Harthill, a pretty village a couple of miles from Killamarsh, but Eileen and Wendy's mother still lived in the village and she was a customer of mine. Talk about different generations. Wendy congratulated Alistair and Louise on all they had done regards the rooftop protest and said how proud we all were of them both. "Alistair, have you anything to report?" asked Wendy.

"SARP are threatening to restart the incinerator. I have a press release from the Ken Coates office; it is not due to go out till tomorrow. It reads, 'How can you restart the incinerator when emergency procedures are not in place? What should residents of Killamarsh and surrounding areas do in the event of another emergency at the SARP plant in the village?' local Euro MP Ken Coates has asked the company and its owners, the French multinational Vivendi. Mr. Coates is tonight participating in a special meeting in the village which will finalise details for the presentation of a petition of over 3,300 signatures. The petition, which was collected in less than a week by Residents Against SARP Pollution (RASP), demands that the incinerator remains closed. Mr. Coates is arranging for a copy to go next week to the Petitions Committee of the European Parliament in Strasbourg. In his letter to the President of Vivendi, M. Jean-Marie Messier, Mr. Coates says, "I write to you on a matter of great urgency concerning the SARP plant at Killamarsh. When I met Philippe Martin (the head of SARP Industries) in Strasbourg in June, I was very pleased when he told me that the company were voluntarily going to implement the Seveso Directive on the control of major accidents with respect to Killamarsh. This, of course, entails the setting in place of detailed off-site emergency procedures, as well as plans to deal with emergencies inside the plant. The work on the necessary emergency measures is not yet complete," says Mr. Coates. "Yet I understand that SARP intend to restart the chemical waste incinerator this week using diesel oil. This is very worrying to local residents and myself. Surely it is inappropriate to restart the incinerator before the emergency drills have been finalised? I have also raised my concerns about restarting the incinerator at Killamarsh with the European Environmental Commissioner, Mrs. Bjerregaard, says Mr. Coates. "In the circumstances, shouldn't the restarting of the chemical waste incinerator be put on hold, at least until all the safety audits have been completed and the emergency procedures are securely in place?""'"

Alistair put the press release down on the table. "We have been asked by Ken Coates if one of the group will fly to Strasbourg to present the petition on behalf of RASP. Who do we want to go to Strasbourg on our behalf?" The most popular choice was our technical expert, Ian Legge, who worked mostly behind the scenes and didn't always get the recognition he was due. "OK, Ian, if you are available we will book your flight to Strasbourg."

Wendy asked if there was anything else.

"Yes, there is." It was Ian Legge. "I have something that I think we should look into. Our research team have been checking through public records compiled by the Environment Agency, and we have found that a delivery of 20 tonnes of deadly arsenic was delivered to SARP UK. As they were not allowed to handle arsenic under their licence, where is it now? Have they put it through the incinerator before the incinerator was shut down? We have found traces of it in the emission recordings and that is what made us check to see if if any arsenic had been delivered to the site. No other arsenic has been recorded on the public record for January to June this year other than the 191-ton tanker load."

The question was clear. They had 20 tonnes of arsenic: where was it?

I was collecting on the milk round on November 12. I had almost finished. I was on the Norwood Estate, not far from the SARP site; the estate stands on a hill and has a clear view of the incinerator and the SARP plant. At the house of one of my customers, a man named Johnny, he said he wanted to talk about barrels hidden in the ground on the SARP site. Johnny had run his own small transport business and he had regularly been used by Leigh prior to SARP taking over last January.

He told me, "You know, John, that the site is built on the old Norwood pit, there is a maze of tunnels running from there under Killamarsh. In the 90s I would bring barrels from different Leigh Environmental sites. I would reverse on to the site to a particular place covered by steel covers. They would remove the covers and I was instructed to tip; the barrels would disappear. On more than one occasion I asked, 'Where do they go?' I always got the same answer. 'Oh, we just store them down there.' Over the years the steel covers moved from place to place, they were tipping into the old mineshafts. Killamarsh sits on a toxic lake, that's why they get so many terrible smells everywhere from the grids in the village. That apart, what I want to tell you is that when they were building the new administration block in the early '90s I saw in the foundations row after row of old barrels full of chemicals laid in trenches and then covered in. I can go to the site and I will show you where they are buried."

"Thanks," I said to him, "I will be back in touch." With that I climbed back into my VW Transporter and made my way home.

The next day I contacted Alan Charles and arranged a meeting for 7.00 pm that night, Friday 13. I retold the story of the contractor, and Alan asked if we could arrange a meeting with Johnny at the site to pinpoint the position of the buried barrels. I said that I would do that. I returned that night to see Johnny and he said that on Sunday morning at 10.00 am he would meet Alan Charles and myself at SARP UK and show us the spot.

On the Sunday morning, November 15, the three of us met up at the SARP gates, close to the administration block. "That's the spot," Johnny said, pointing to the building. "When they were putting down the foundations, there was a forklift truck driver dropping barrel after barrel into them. I asked the guy on the forklift what was in them, and 'Nothing much,' was his reply. But I had noticed that they were all covered with skull and crossbones stickers. I was shocked."

We both thanked Johnny. Alan Charles was the first to drive away and, as I went to follow him, Johnny shouted to me, "Have you got a few minutes, John? There was something else I wanted to show you."

We walked round the perimeter fence, then walked through the fence, as the holes were still there. Johnny pointed to three separate areas of concrete, each about five metres square. "That's where I used to drop the barrels, where the steel sheets used to be, covering the mineshafts to the old Norwood Pit."

At that moment my thoughts went back to the two mysterious flat-back wagons that had always parked up near this spot once every week, covered by tarpaulins, having arrived in the early hours. Their identity and origin was completely unknown until one of my milk lads scaled the fence, turned back the tarpaulin, and saw that the transport company's address was a village situated close to the Sellafield nuclear power station in Cumbria. The implications were obvious.

I thanked Johnny once again as we returned to our cars, then we both drove away.

The following week, our discovery of the buried barrels was leaked to the press and made it into *The Yorkshire Post*.

Rob Waugh wrote, "Drums of chemicals have been illegally buried in the ground at the controversial SARP UK waste recycling plant, it is claimed. The allegations date back to when the Killamarsh based plant was owned by Leigh Environmental, which was taken over by SARP last year. A government watchdog, the Environment Agency, are to investigate. *The Yorkshire Post* understands that a contractor working on the site eight years ago claimed he saw drums of chemicals laid in trenches ready to be buried. The allegations have been made in person to Derbyshire County Councillor Alan Charles. The exact site where drums are allegedly buried has been pinpointed and the County Council has asked the EA to investigate. The claims have alarmed Coun. Charles and the action group that is campaigning to close the plant because of its safety record. Coun. Charles said, 'I want to substantiate whether this is true and would have a great deal of concern if it is. It would then beg the question of whether there is anything else buried there that shouldn't be.'

"A spokesman for Residents Against SARP Pollution (RASP), John Moran, said the group was horrified by the allegations and was anxious that the EA carried out the fullest investigation. Mr. Moran said, 'Everybody at RASP is extremely concerned that the previous owners could have dumped barrels of chemicals in the ground. If this is true, they must have had a reason for doing so and we must know what is buried down there. If the barrels are found it puts the whole safety of the site into doubt.'

"A spokesman for the Environment Agency said, 'We have received a letter from the Derbyshire County Council Planning Dept. today which concerns an anonymous complaint made to them with a reference to a 100-metre stretch of the site at Killamarsh. This is a matter we are taking very seriously, at this stage we need more information before we go on site.'

"Last night SARP issued a statement saying it was aware of the allegations but had no factual evidence to support the claims. It is understood that the drums which have allegedly been buried will be discussed tomorrow night at the regular liaison meeting between the local elected councillors and the Environment Agency."

Chapter Seventeen

Strasbourg and Brussels

On the same day as the meeting with Alan Charles, RASP issued a press release. Although the trip had been suggested by Ken Coates MEP, who had also organised various meetings with European politicians, Ian's travel was paid for by the funds of RASP, showing that we were a group to be reckoned with.

THE CAMPAIGN TO CLOSE SARP UK GOES TO EUROPE
Whilst visiting the European Parliament buildings in Brussels and Strasbourg, RASP member Ian Legge presented both the petition seeking SARP UK closure and RASP's very strong and reasoned objections to the company's integrated pollution control application presented to the Environment Agency. A very senior official of the Environment Commission, a cabinet member, received him in Brussels.

Great understanding was demonstrated of the unacceptable current position. Pertinent advice was offered of how community law can be of assistance. It was noted that Vivendi, the parent company of SARP UK, has recently spent billions of dollars acquiring profitable American power generators and this was compared with the insignificant investment in apparently essential plant for safe working at Killamarsh. Ken Coates, the region's MEP, also arranged for meetings with various other MEPs in Strasbourg; it was noticeable how knowledgeable and sympathetic people are regarding the RASP campaign and encouragement and advice were offered.

On Monday November 16, I arrived at the Crown as usual for the weekly meeting. Wendy opened proceedings and congratulated Ian Legge on his visit to Strasbourg and Brussels, and how well he had been received. "Alistair, I know you have two protests that you are organising this week – can you let us know what they are?"

"Firstly, I would like us to visit the Environment Agency at Rotherham and take the petition, which has 5,000 signatures opposing the reopening of the incinerator. And I would like to arrange it for Wednesday morning at 10.00 am, can we have a show of hands who can make it?" About 30 hands went up, but we could always double that so we could expect around 60; that would do fine.

"Secondly, I would like to organise another protest outside the gates for Thursday morning about 9.00 am." A similar number of hands went up when asked, so 60 at each was OK.

On the Wednesday morning, November 18, it was indeed around 60 protesters who arrived at Templeborough, Rotherham. We brought all our banners and placards, the EA had never seen the likes before on their doorstep. We did not trust the EA. They had not protected our village when they should have from years of pollution and problems from Leigh/SARP, and if we were not watching them as close as we were watching SARP, they would not be doing so now. We presented our 5,000-signature petition to manager of the EA John Houseman. We then were invited into the main office, where RASP members quizzed Inspector Colin Guest and John Houseman about SARP restarting the incinerator. They confirmed that they were responsible for the tightening up of the emission levels that SARP were not allowed to exceed with the incinerator.

I said, "It's RASP's opinion that SARP cannot keep within these limits with the incinerator they have got at this site, do you agree? And secondly, if they don't, when will you get the readings when they trial it with diesel?"

Colin Guest was the first to answer. "The answer to the first question is that it could be possible if SARP has installed the proper equipment, if not then it's not likely."

I asked, "Is the proper equipment the one costing £1 million or is it the one costing £335,000?"

"The one costing £1 million would be needed. The answer to your second question is the next day, we will be taking readings off the incinerator on a daily basis."

"Well, in that case," I said, "SARP UK will never be able to use that incinerator again, because RASP knows that they will never spend the million."

John Houseman and Colin Guest then amazed the RASP members by saying, "We don't want to be picking SARP UK up on all the points raised by the RASP group for fear of harassment charges being levelled at the EA."

Colin Guest admitted that documentation for the "Three Tipper Loads" was not in order, but admitted that they had so far taken no action.

Brian Ashmore asked John Houseman why the EA were once again not coming out to the site when a complaint was made, it was slipping back to the way it was before. He replied that they were short of staff and had to prioritise.

Peter Gurney responded by saying, "That is not good enough. We will be in touch with your boss Michael Meacher; he will get it sorted."

We Shall Not Be Moved. Some of the hardcore of the RASP group in our customary position outside the gates of SARP. Brian Ashmore in his signature beret is standing at the back, while Sandra and I are at the right of the front row. The day of this protest would see the arrest of one of our number, Steve Birch, although the police decided not to go to the trouble of arresting all of us! The cheerful expressions on many faces in this photo show the high morale and camaraderie that we had.

Front row, from left: Margaret Marsh, June Cullabine, Carol Dye, Ann Cockerill, Allison Sampson, Margaret Parr, John Moran, Sandra Moran

Top row, from left: Margaret Ashmore, Brenda Glossop (turning to keep an eye on SARP UK), Brian Ashmore, May Hobson, Avril Gold, Trevor Cockerill, Terry Hobson and David Parr

John Houseman and Colin Guest were looking very uncomfortable. We had long had our doubts about the EA, and no wonder after these latest admissions. It was a good job we hadn't been bothered about "harassment charges" or RASP wouldn't have got very far against SARP UK. The meeting ended. We had raised more questions than answers, we would have to follow them up.

At 8.45 am on November 19 the protesters were there at the gates of SARP, around 70 in total. With the famous banner proclaiming "Residents Against SARP Pollution" standing behind us, the protesters sat down across the road. Steve Birch was on the extreme left, then Margaret Marsh, June Cullabine, Carol Dye, Ann Cockerill, Allison Sampson, Margaret Parr, myself and Sandra.

Carol Dye led the singing. "We shall not be moved!" The words echoed on the cold morning air, everyone sat there defiantly as the Derbyshire constabulary, out in force, moved towards us. The singing continued, not one person moved.

"You will be arrested if you do not clear the highway and allow these tankers through."

Still no one moved and the singing went on. The officer that had just given the ultimatum retreated back to his colleagues, of which there were maybe 15 or so. I had never been so proud to sit next to eight very brave people. These included a person that I had once thought of as a bit soft – Allison. I couldn't have got it more wrong.

The stalemate was broken by the arrival of Parish Councillors Jayne Holden and Bob Harper, who had come to a meeting arranged by SARP UK about restarting the incinerator. The pair walked towards the gate, "Lady Jayne" in her finery.

"Blimey, Jayne, for a second I thought you were going to join us," Carol Dye said, looking up from the ground.

With a toss of her long blonde hair Lady Jayne passed the protesters as if they were not there. One thing was for sure, Lady Jayne would never lower herself to such actions, but it was these same protesters on the road that morning who had kept this toxic plant from operating this last six months, something Jayne Holden and all the other councillors had failed to achieve over the last 20 years.

As the Parish Councillors disappeared into the offices, the police once more came towards us. Steve Birch, who was on the end, was grabbed by two big constables, frogmarched to the riot van and put under arrest. We continued to sing, "We shall not, we shall not be moved!"

The police realised that they would have to arrest us all, that was not what they wanted, as all the TV cameras and press were watching. We continued singing and after another 20 minutes we ended our protest and slowly and I thought with great dignity folded our huge white banner away.

It was the following Monday at the Crown, November 23. We had started to use the smaller main lounge for the meetings now – the heady days of 200 at meetings were long gone. We now had around 25 really committed RASP protesters, supported by another 35 who were not so committed but could always be relied upon for protests and the like. The much colder weather and foggy nights were here now, but we always had around 35 at the meetings still.

Wendy as usual congratulated the success of the protesters; both protests had been well covered by the media and as yet there had been no trial of the incinerator prior to restarting, we were going into the seventh month soon and it had still not been lit. It was "a wonderful achievement" in the words of RASP's friend MEP Ken Coates.

"Ian, what do you propose we do about the 'lost arsenic'?" was Wendy's next question.

"Well, I think that we should write to them and if they cannot give a good explanation, go to the press. I think John will be OK with that."

I nodded. SARP UK had certainly battened down the hatches, they had become extra careful, they knew that we would punish them for the slightest error, and at the moment they were just about succeeding.

"I will write the letter, keep a few copies and send it by Recorded delivery to SARP UK, Ellisons Road, Norwood Industrial Estate, Killamarsh," said Ian.

On Tuesday November 24, I wrote to Harry Barnes MP over the points raised on our visit to the Environment Agency at Templeborough, Rotherham.

Dear Harry,

I am writing on behalf of RASP. We are very concerned at events relating to the SARP UK plant at Killamarsh and the Environment Agency. As you are aware, a delegation from RASP on Wednesday November 18 presented the EA at Rotherham with a 5,000-name petition requesting that the incinerator at SARP UK would not be restarted until:

1. All variations to licence objections had been dealt with

2. ECUS (Sheffield University) audit had been completed

3. There had been a full public enquiry.

After the presentation at the Environment Agency we were invited into their offices, where we held discussions with John Houseman and Colin Guest. We were most concerned with what we heard; they stated that they did not want to be picking SARP UK up on points raised by our campaign group for fear of harassment charges being levelled at them by SARP. This statement ties in with the latest allegations by RASP. We have reliable information from the inside that a substantial number of barrels of "Almost untreatable" type chemicals are buried on this site.

We have brought this to the attention of Alan Charles, our Derbyshire County Councillor, who has informed the county planning office at Matlock. At a recent meeting, the informant concerned pinpointed the exact spot. The result of that meeting was that the EA were informed and, according to Alan Charles, to quote, "The EA did not attach as much importance as RASP and himself to the findings of these barrels as they did not seem to impose any danger where they were."

This matter was discussed at the liaison meeting with SARP on Tuesday evening. We at RASP cannot understand this attitude of what we see as a desire not to investigate this site or this company. This follows previous allegations against Leigh Environmental over alleged "misuse" of their landfill by illegal tipping. The EA admitted that documentation for the "Three Tipper Loads" was not in order but on the tipping and documentation nothing has been done. Added to this is the third point that RASP members and the general public of Killamarsh are continually contacting us to tell us that there is no response from the EA to complaints against the company regards foul smells etc. Either "no response" or "too late" seems to be the case. Mr. Michael Meacher, in the debate with yourself on October 21, stated that there was sufficient legislation in place and he expects the EA to enforce it. Can you on our behalf raise our concerns with him at the earliest opportunity?

John Moran (RASP)

Today, Wednesday November 25, we arranged a Spade Protest. We all arrived, about 40 of us, at the gates of SARP UK carrying spades and shovels, we had all the media there. We explained to the press that we had brought these spades as a reminder to the Environment Agency that we would dig for them to find the missing drums.

The headlines in *The Sheffield Star* that same day, and *The Yorkshire Post* on the following day, were, "RASP DIGS UP A FUSS".

However, that was not all that was going on in the press at that time. On Friday November 27 in *The Daily Telegraph* Vivendi had taken a complete full-page advertisement. Half the page was a coloured jigsaw, the lower half a young girl with a scarf partly covering her face. Then came the following lines: "Imagine a world which gets progressively cleaner. Imagine a world where new forms of communications technology are more user friendly. Vivendi has already imagined this world. What is more, we have begun to build it. Reading this you might deduce that such wide-ranging activities are commensurate with considerable financial growth. And you would be right. Vivendi is one of the largest companies in

Europe, with an annual turnover approaching £21 billion. All things considered, it seems that when the customer comes first, success soon follows. COMMITTED TO MEETING YOUR LIFE'S EVER-CHANGING NEEDS."

The old saying "What can't speak can't lie" was, in the view of RASP, stretched to breaking point in *The Daily Telegraph*.

The trials of the incinerator with diesel oil had not materialised. We had been holding almost daily protests at the SARP gates throughout the month, and now we didn't expect SARP to restart the incinerator until after Christmas, nothing to do with "Goodwill to All Men" but we thought that they were very concerned at the level of scrutiny that was on them.

Chapter Eighteen

Yorkshire Television Story of the Year

The end of a momentous year was approaching, and this was marked in one way by a trip I made on December 16 to the Yorkshire Television Studios in Leeds for their Calendar News programme. RASP and the campaign had been named the "Calendar News Story of the Year" for 1998.

It was a bitterly cold day as we made our way up the M1. The snow and rain were blowing off the Pennines and the driving was quite difficult. On entering the television studios I was directed by a young lady to the makeup department – yes, even middle-aged milkmen get the treatment before going in front of the cameras.

Christa Ackroyd and Mike Morris were the presenters on the programme and it was Christa who did the interview. She started by saying, "There is a story that seems to have gone on longer than any other in our region this year; I am talking about a small ex-mining village in North East Derbyshire, who took on the might of the French multinational company Vivendi, I am of course talking about Killamarsh and the environmental campaign group RASP, or to give them their proper name, Residents Against SARP Pollution. Tonight I welcome John Moran, the press officer for that group.

"Well, John, you don't look like a typical campaigner; you sit here in your smart suit and tie, but its not always like that, is it? We have seen you and your fellow campaigners for the last seven or eight months holding up tankers, then going to the company headquarters in Paris, meetings with Environment Ministers, debates in the Houses of Parliament in London and in the European Parliament in Brussels, where you have presented petitions to both. We have seen your fellow protesters stage an early morning rooftop protest and your people arrested. Tell me, John, how did your group become one of the most organised powerful campaign groups that we have ever seen in this area?"

"The only answer to that, Christa, is people in Killamarsh have been poisoned and polluted by Leigh Environmental and then by SARP UK. Then on two days in May there were two clouds too many – the community had had enough. They decided to stand and be counted. They knew from years of suffering caused by these toxic waste companies that we had to take them on. We had to take them on on our own. No one stood with us, not the Derbyshire County or Parish Councils, not the Environment Agency, nor the Education Committee or the local Health Authority. RASP, or Residents Against SARP Pollution, was born because we had no other place to turn."

"Well, John, we think that RASP have been brilliant and we wish you all well in the coming year, 1999."

With that the lights in the studio dimmed, and for the next year the opening footage on every Yorkshire Calendar evening news programme was of RASP protesting outside No. 52 Rue d'Anjou, Paris.

We had not received a reply from SARP UK to the letter that Ian Legge wrote over the 20 tonnes of missing arsenic. Ian spoke to me and we agreed that he should inform the Environment Agency and I would leak the story to the press. On the following day the *Yorkshire Post* headline read: "Lost Arsenic Just a Slip-Up on Our Forms – SARP Pins Blame on Clerical Error". Graham Readfearn went on to write: "A clerical error at a controversial industrial waste plant started a government and European Commission investigation into 20 tonnes of 'lost arsenic'. Politicians and campaigners last night hit out at Killamarsh plant owners SARP UK accusing them of incompetence, but all wanted the company's explanation to be fully investigated.

"Campaign group RASP (Residents Against SARP Pollution) earlier this month asked the company what had happened to a delivery of 20 tonnes of deadly arsenic which appeared on public records compiled by the Environment Agency. After the group failed to get answers, it alerted the Environment Agency, which immediately launched an investigation into the plant at Killamarsh near Sheffield. Euro MP Ken Coates raised the matter in Brussels with the European Environment Commissioner Ritt Bjerregaard, who has been monitoring investigations into two toxic leaks at SARP.

"But last night the company said it had sent the wrong information to the Agency about deliveries in April of this year. Code H43 was used by mistake to describe a tanker-load of 'spent sodium hyperchlorite', a substance similar to household bleach. A SARP spokesman said, 'This is actually our fault, the girl who has filled in the form had made a mistake, which is not good on our part.' *The Yorkshire Post* was shown documents sent to the Environment Agency which illustrated the glaring error. No other 'arsenic' had been recorded on the public hazardous waste record for January to June this year other than the 19.7-ton tanker-load.

"Mr. Coates said, 'This is a very alarming failure in record-keeping. If this does prove to be the true explanation, a lot of people's time and effort will have been wasted. We need to have more confidence in record-keeping at SARP UK – the company cannot go on like this.'

"North East Derbyshire MP Harry Barnes said, 'These things need to be investigated carefully, there is a tremendous distrust of the plant within the community and what they are finding out about the operations of the company are not something to enthuse them with a great deal of confidence.'

"Ian Legge, a qualified chemist who investigated the 'lost' arsenic as a member of the campaign group RASP, said, 'Can we believe this explanation? I think the Environment Agency also have some explaining to do as to why this has happened at all.' An EA spokeswoman said, 'We are now waiting for SARP's explanation in writing. We would want to fully investigate this explanation before we comment.'"

On December 18, RASP member Steve Birch appeared in Chesterfield Magistrates' Court, charged with wilful obstruction of the highway. He was fined £50, which was paid for by RASP.

Three days later, RASP issued the following press release in relation to the mystery of the buried drums.

SONAR SEARCH FOR DRUMS
SARP backtracked today in the search for the "buried" drums. They said last week that they needed to have "factual evidence" before they would dig. They today have agreed to a

request by the EA to bring in a specialist team with sonar equipment to search the site.

RASP spokesman John Moran said, "We believe the pressure of the press and our continued hammering of the Agency has forced them to dig."

SARP UK have announced that they are shutting down all operations till January.

"We will keep a token force here at different times of the day just in case this company uses the time to do anything illegal, and then we will resume the protests as soon as they restart in the new year."

The trialling of the incinerator has been put on hold until January.

SARP UK returned to work on January 4, 1999, and we were there to meet them. The Toxic Night Shift were once more watching SARP, the 24-hour watch was back on. I joined the members of the Toxic Night Shift down at the gates, Ann Nettleship and her sister June Cullabine were there as usual, Sandra, Allison Sampson and Ann Cockerill.

"When do you think they are going to restart the incinerator, John?" asked June.

"I think they will try to restart in the next week or so, they are only burning diesel oil, but it will definitely be under the cover of darkness, so as soon as you see smoke, we will want to know, so that we can log any smells or black smoke. That is a sign that they are exceeding the limits."

It was a week later we started to hear the rumours, and soon after the stories started to emerge in the press, like in this article by Martin Fisher of *The Derbyshire Times*, headlined "Blighted Firm Staying Put Say Bosses – Closure Rumour Denied by SARP Chiefs." He wrote: "Bosses at Killamarsh chemical company SARP have denied rumours that the blighted plant is closing down. John Moran, spokesman for pressure group Residents Against SARP Pollution (RASP), claims he has leaked information from the company's head office in Birmingham that the firm is to close in March or April. He also says the company is only giving out short-term six-month contracts instead of 12-month contracts to forklift truck drivers following fears about the future of the site and relocation of the incinerator to Lancashire.

"But a SARP spokesman, Phil Rostance, said the firm was staying put. 'We are not closing at all,' he said, adding that there was no truth in contracts being reduced or that the company was relocating its incinerator. 'We don't employ any forklift truck drivers,' he added. 'We employ contractors who are multi-disciplined.'

"But Mr. Moran said, 'They are going to deny that they are going until the incinerator is down and there is no place to get rid of these toxic wastes. Regards the forklift truck drivers, describing anyone working at this site as "multi-disciplined" even for SARP is beyond belief. We are going to keep up the protests for however long it takes. This company is going to be watched 24 hours a day.'

"SARP's incinerator is due to be working again within the next four weeks, following a series of tests. Mr. Rostance said, 'We listened to the concerns of key representatives and delayed recommencing the high-temperature incinerator until the festive period was over.' He added the incinerator was not connected with the two incidents in May, when thousands of residents were warned to stay indoors.

"Charges against SARP UK by the Health and Safety Executive and the Environment Agency will be heard on February 26, after the hearing was adjourned after the company asked for more time to consider evidence from expert witness for the prosecution. Pleas have yet to be entered to the charges."

Chapter Nineteen

One Man and His Dog

On February 4, 1999, RASP came to the Village Centre in Killamarsh, at which the Minister for Education David Blunkett was due to arrive to officially open the new Community and Learning Opportunity Centre at about 10.00 am. RASP planned to use the visit to further our own cause, knowing that there would be plenty of media coverage. At about 9.45 I arrived at the new centre; already there were around 60 RASP protesters. The weather was absolutely freezing, we were all wrapped up against the cold with woolly hats and thick coats against the biting North East winds, traces of snow on the rock-hard ground from the flurries of the previous night. We were greeted by Lady Jayne and her constant companion Bob Harper of the Parish Council; they were most annoyed at the prospect of anything spoiling their "special day" with David Blunkett.

"What are all you doing here?" was her opening comment.

"We are here, Jayne, to inform the Minister for Education as to the dangers of SARP UK in relation to the two Sheffield Road schools. It may not be the priority for you and the Derbyshire Council but it is for RASP," I replied, before the moment to get back at her was lost.

The whole of the Derbyshire Council were openly hostile to the RASP campaign; even Coun. Alan Charles, our only true supporter, was now strangely silent. He had not been seen to be with us since the Swallow Hotel press conference. The half-page photograph of him between me and Alistair in *The Yorkshire Post* had been rumoured not to have gone down well with his bosses at County Hall in Matlock.

RASP campaigners moved to virtually block the entrance to the new building, as the large black chauffeur-driven Daimler glided to a stop. David Blunkett, accompanied by his black Labrador guide dog, emerged from the rear door. To the horrified looks of the awaiting Parish Councillors we moved around him.

"Mr. Blunkett, what is your position regarding the safety of the Sheffield Road schools if SARP UK restart their incinerator?" shouted Ann Cockerill.

Taken aback slightly, the blind Minister stopped despite the officials trying to hurry him into the building. "I am aware of the feelings in the village about this toxic waste plant and the history, especially over the last 12 months, in regard to its proximity to the two schools on the Sheffield Road, but this matter is in the hands of Health and Safety and the Environment Agency and as this in the middle of court proceedings it would be inappropriate to comment."

"Stop sitting on the fence, Blunkett, you are the Minister of Education, do something!" Carol Dye responded angrily.

Many more were now crowding the Minister, and at this point the Derbyshire constabulary moved in and escorted him into the entrance foyer of the new building. The whole scene had been filmed by BBC and ITV and witnessed by the media. We would have full coverage of David Blunkett's visit, but in the eyes of Jayne Holden and her Parish Councillors for the wrong reasons.

When Blunkett emerged an hour later we were still there. Throughout his time inside the constant protest songs would have been clearly heard by him.

Ian Legge spoke as he was about to get into the Daimler. "Minister, we would like to present you with this petition, signed by 6,000 Killamarsh residents opposing the restarting of the incinerator at SARP UK."

Taking the petition, he said, "I would like to say that I have great sympathy with all the parents over this issue, but as I have already said another government department has this matter in hand, and we must leave it for their decision." With that the Minister's chauffeur closed the back door, returned to his front seat and the black Daimler slid away.

The phone rang at 10.20 pm on Monday February 20. It was Allison Sampson. "John, we are outside the gates at SARP, we can see smoke coming from the incinerator."

My heart dropped. Even though we had been expecting it for months, the satisfaction that we had stopped them using it for 10 months was over. It was a giant step backwards for us all to take. "I will be down in five minutes, Allison."

At that moment as I replaced the telephone receiver Sandra came in, having just finished her shift at Derwent House. "SARP's just started up again, I am going down," I told her.

"Hang on, I'm coming with you," she replied.

As we approached, we could clearly see the smoke coming from the incinerator. "God, what a horrible sight," were Sandra's only words as we pulled up at the gates. There were around 20 RASP protesters; most of them had been there every night since the reopening on January 4.

"It looks very dark, the smoke, John," was Ian Legge's observation.

"Yes, I would say that it does not look right," I replied.

The group, under Ian Legge's guidance, had become expert at the colour that the incinerator should and shouldn't emit. We knew that the smoke should be clear, otherwise it was not burning the material properly, and the temperatures needed were not being achieved.

The incinerator continued to burn through the night.

The next day, Ian Legge was in touch to get the readings. As usual, the Environment Agency had not received the readings from SARP despite the promise to the group that we would be given them the next day.

John Houseman, the EA manager at Templeborough in Rotherham, made some excuse but said he would be on to it, and would report back to Ian and RASP in the next few days.

The incinerator burned diesel oil as part of the testing process every night that week until Friday, February 24, when we at RASP, standing in freezing temperatures and light drizzle, watched the incinerator and realised they had not fired it up that night. It stayed unlit. Why?

On the next Monday I arrived at the Crown, on a night so cold and foggy that only dedicated campaigners would turn out. The meeting heard from Ian Legge, who had had the results back from the Environment Agency.

Ian began, "The EA has today sent us the results of the trialing of the incinerator between Monday February 20 and

Thursday 23. They show that the incinerator emissions were exceeded at sometime or other in every hour on each of the nights. I would say, ladies and gentlemen, that SARP UK are having serious problems with their incinerator."

The 40 campaigners in the Crown made as much noise as the 200 had made almost a year ago. As the applause died down, Wendy Wellings turned to me and asked. "John, would you like to say anything?"

I stood up and this was my reply, "Thanks to Ian and his team, great work. I believe that SARP UK were never going to keep to the new emission levels set last year. I don't think they will ever be able to do so – time will tell."

The meeting ended with all the campaigners in great heart, we could see a light at the end of tunnel.

That Thursday, February 23, 1999 would prove to be the last time that a toxic waste incinerator would pollute our village.

The days of March and the lighter nights saw the protesters still at the gates of SARP UK and the Toxic Night Shift continued to monitor 24 hours a day. The place was now very quiet, transport had been vastly reduced, the incinerator had not restarted, the acid plant and oil plant were all gone. Only the secondary liquid fuel plant remained. We wanted this process shut down as well and then SARP UK would have nothing left, the only problem, and we knew it, was Derbyshire County Council would lose all their funding.

On Thursday March 20, Dr. Dick van Steenis, the country's leading medical expert on toxic incinerators and their effects on human health, came to the Village Centre at the invitation of RASP. The place was packed. Sharing the platform with Dr. van Steenis were Alan Charles and Ken Coates MEP, who was acting as Chairperson.

Ken Coates introduced Dr. van Steenis, and the doctor began speaking. "I would like to ask you a question. Why do the poor die younger than the rich? There are many explanations and most point to the lifestyle of the less well-off part of our society. They eat the wrong foods, smoke too much and don't exercise enough. Recently we learnt that, whilst all these factors are doubtless important, one of the deadliest killers has been largely overlooked. The poor die younger because in certain parts of the UK they are being systematically poisoned. In 1994, as a retired GP, I was asked to look into possible health effects of pollution from power stations in South Wales. We used a simple device of mapping the use of asthma inhalers by primary school children. I was astonished to discover that before long I was able to predict the number of asthma patients to within one or two percent, simply by measuring how far they lived from the nearest major source of pollution. In some villages, I found as many as 38 percent of four and five-year-olds using inhalers.

"I started to use this simple test. In Lancashire I found that six times as many inhalers were used downwind of the cement works than were used upwind. Whilst government monitoring equipment was showing scarcely credible readings of minus 17 microgrammes of smoke particles per cubic metre of air, unofficial monitors in a nearby school playground found levels as high as 485 microgrammes, or nine times the Government's 'safe limit'."

The information supplied by the Derbyshire Health Authority that the asthma and use of inhalers in Killamarsh was about average, if not below, was looking extremely fragile. Was it another case of covering up? Most of the audience were sure that was the case and the findings of the doctor only seemed to confirm what we had all known all along.

The doctor continued, "While the number of Britain's factories has declined over the last 40 years, pollutants have greatly increased. The main reason is that we are generating more waste. It is either being dumped in landfill sites where pollutants can react with each other to produce more deadly ones, or being incinerated in incinerators like the one in your village at SARP UK. Since 1991, companies have been allowed to burn toxic wastes to power industrial processes. It's not hard to see why they want to do this – while coal costs £26 per tonne they are paid to take poisonous chemicals away. But because the chemicals are classed as 'fuel' rather than waste, they are not required to fit proper scrubbing equipment to their chimneys. In the last 12 months the UK's largest factories released over 10,000 tonnes of cancer-causing chemicals into the air. The result is a huge increase in certain diseases. I link the rise of endometriosis – a horrible, painful condition now afflicting as many as 10 percent of the population – to the emissions of dioxins, which are common toxic byproducts of incineration. Hypothyroidism, which is now becoming epidemic in the UK, seems to be linked to volatile organic compounds, whilst the heavy metals have been blamed for cancer, heart disease and strokes.

"In two villages near where I live in South Wales, the infant mortality levels at 12 per 1,000 approach those of Belarus in the aftermath of the Chernobyl disaster. A recent study by Friends of the Earth shows how pollution has become the companion of poverty. 662 of the UK's largest factories are in places in which the average household income is less than £15,000, five are in places whose average income is more than £30,000. Where poverty is most concentrated, so are the poisons. Seal Sands on Teeside contains 17 of Britain's most polluting factories and has an average income of just £6,200."

To a standing ovation, the doctor took a sip of the water in front of him, nodded to the audience and sat down. He looked far from well and as he was now in his later years, he did well to travel the country attending campaign meetings and conferences.

His reference to Seal Sands on Teesside brought back memories of a visit that Sandra and I made up the coast from Whitby where we had been for the day. I have seen some terrible places, but Seal Sands was miles and miles of lunar landscape, with many tall incinerators burning, flames clearly seen coming from the tops, through the mist of that late November day. I will never forget it, my sympathies for the residents of the area could not be overestimated.

Ken Coates thanked the doctor and after he had answered questions for the next half an hour, Ken asked if there was anything else. Ann Nettleship was on her feet.

"I would like to ask Derbyshire County Councillor Alan Charles what was his and the Council's view regards what the doctor said." Ann was clearly keen to find out where the Council stood and more to the point our erstwhile supporter Alan Charles.

Alan Charles rose to his feet. "The position of the Derbyshire County Council is that of my own, it is that SARP's pollution is the same as the effects of people smoking and that I would not, as would my County Council not, vote for the plant to be closed if it cost the Council money."

At this, the doctor was back on his feet. "There is no comparison between passive smoking and the toxic poisons from these industrial incinerators – that is quite absurd that you and your Council can harbour such ideas."

Ann Nettleship and RASP now had our answer: Alan Charles had done a complete turnaround. He had been through so many protests with us, to SARP, Paris and the Swallow Hotel, but we now seemed to have gone our separate ways. To many jibes of "Judas" from the ranks of the RASP campaigners, the meeting broke up. The only unanswered question over Alan Charles was why had he done it?

It was Friday April 2, 1999. The phone rang as I was just about to go collecting on the milk round. "Margaret Ashmore here, John. I am at the SARP gates and something is going off, they have been evacuating staff off the site to near the administration block, but at the moment we are not sure what is happening."

"OK, Margaret, I will get onto the press and they will find out what is going on. Will speak later; if anything else happens let me know." I put the phone down and rang Rob Waugh on the news desk at *The Yorkshire Post*. The next day's edition ran the headline "Waste Plant in New Toxic Leak Alert" above an article that read: "The troubled SARP UK waste recycling plant near Sheffield is facing a fresh investigation after another leak of toxic chemicals. The Environment Agency confirmed that poisonous fumes escaped from a storage container at the plant in Killamarsh leading to a partial evacuation of the site. Vapour from the leak of butyl acrylate could be smelt several hundred yards away in the Rother Valley Country Park, where members of the public raised the alarm. A spokeswomen for the agency said the leak was a 'serious issue' and added that there was concern that the company had not informed them as soon as the danger became apparent. The latest in a string of safety breaches at the site happened after the container was left out in the warm sunlight. It expanded and split. After the company discovered the leak, staff were moved away from the area to an administration block to avoid the fumes, which can cause respiratory problems. Environment Agency staff then helped SARP personnel make the container safe.

"The agency spokeswoman said, 'The chemicals are used in textiles and are toxic and flammable. The company had to make sure that staff were moved away from the part of the site – breathing in the fumes can cause a tightening in the chest and choking. We will be wanting to know why the company did not report it to us straightaway and we will be investigating how much chemical was leaked.'

"A SARP spokesman said that the company didn't directly inform the agency because one of its officers happened to be due for a meeting at the site around the time of the leak on Thursday afternoon. He added, 'Appropriate safety action was taken to resolve the situation. No workers were put at risk and no damage caused to the environment.'"

Chapter Twenty

Protesters Go to the Polls

The following Monday at the Crown Wendy Wellings opened the meeting by asking, "Alistair, have you anything planned for the next week?"

"Yes, I have. On May 6, the Parish Council elections are due to be held. I think that RASP should put up independent candidates. We have lots of support in the village and Labour has never been challenged as long as anyone can remember. It would mean that we could get representation on the SARP/Parish Council meetings, which would be important. Tonight I want to know if anyone is up for it?"

The hands started to go up for potential councillors and eight names were put forward.

The following day's headlines in the *Star* and *The Yorkshire Post* were the same: "Protesters Go to the Polls."

The *Sheffield Star* went on to say, "Labour faces its biggest challenge for years in its Killamarsh stronghold in the upcoming district and parish elections. No fewer than eight prominent members of the RASP campaign group are standing as independent candidates. 'We are far from happy with the way the Parish and the District Councils have backed our campaign to close down SARP UK,' said John Moran at the launch of the election campaign on Wednesday morning. He went on to say, 'These eight people have been with us since the start of the campaign 12 months ago and have been on every protest. The biggest issue in the village at the moment is SARP UK and we believe that if the Labour Party will not lead us to close the plant, we must look to our own party to do it.' RASP District Council candidates are Carol Dye, Ian Legge, Kevin Sampson and Terry Turner. These together with Ann Cockerill, Sandra Moran, Allison Sampson and Louise Wellings are standing for the Parish Council. In Killamarsh there are 15 parish and four district seats; they will be contested on May 6."

The following Monday at the Crown, Wendy Wellings opened the meeting by asking Alistair for an update on the upcoming Council elections.

"The Parish Council campaign is going well, we have posters on virtually every lamppost and in windows all over village."

The orange and green posters were everywhere, they read:

FOR KILLAMARSH
VOTE RASP.
FOR SARP UK
VOTE ANYONE ELSE.
In the local elections May 6.

When Robert Browning uttered the words, "Oh to be in England now that April's here," he definitely wasn't stood at the perimeter fence at SARP UK in Killamarsh, but that was where RASP campaigners found themselves around 7.00 am on April 11, 1999, a lovely day when the first signs of spring were making themselves felt.

Ever since the court case against Alistair and Louise on November 3 we had kept SARP UK under close scrutiny, not only with the Toxic Night Shift but members patrolling the perimeter of the site, inspecting the security fence that went all the way round the site. What we found didn't bode well for SARP. The same holes that our solicitor Danny Simpson photographed back in November, which had led to a dismissal of the charges against Alistair and Louise, were still unrepaired. Today was the day that RASP would remind

SARP UK why we didn't trust them. Their work practices and security maintenance were appalling and we were going to expose them once again.

Just after dawn, 15 RASP members found themselves at the perimeter fence that led across to the toxic landfill. There, sure enough, were the holes. They simply walked through. They stood on top of the landfill and unfurled a huge banner that read, "FENCE A JOKE".

The next morning *The Yorkshire Post* ran a half-page report with a photo of the banner taken through one of the holes in the perimeter fence and a group of RASP members stood behind it. It was reported that SARP accused RASP of cutting the fence. We responded by saying the holes were the same that had been there in November. By this time of the campaign everyone knew SARP always lied, we at RASP had always told the truth.

By April 21, we had campaigned for almost a year against SARP UK. A lot of RASP supporters had inevitably dropped away for various reasons, mostly trying to find the time when lots of them had families and commitments. This left the real core of RASP, always there at every protest, like the Toxic Night Shift who were always on the SARP gates 24 hours a day. We had already noticed the recent absence of County Councillor Alan Charles, who had apparently been told to toe the party line. It would also appear that Derbyshire County Council rewarded those who did as they are told. That day a press release announced that Alan Charles had been made Head of Education for Derbyshire.

The following Sunday lunchtime at the Crown, Alan Charles ordered a pint and, withdrawing a congratulations telegram from his pocket, asked Roger Barraclough, landlord and vice chairman of RASP, "Who could have sent me that, Roger?"

The card had champagne corks popping on the front cover; on the inside it read, "Well Done, Alan – Some Job, Some Betrayal!" It was signed "RASP".

Roger, as all good landlords do, said nothing,

May 6 was an important day in the life of RASP. That day we created another first for a group such as ours, to stand candidates in the local District and Parish Council elections. Never in anyone's memory had this ever been done before in the United Kingdom. We put up four members for the District and four for the Parish Council. That evening, May 6, 1999, was when history would be made.

We all made our way to the Village Centre. The place was heaving, hundreds having made their way there. Never had local elections in Killamarsh created such interest. At a little after 9.30 pm the votes were being counted. The Labour

Parish Councillors were looking very anxious, this was the first time in many years that they had been opposed at the polls and they were far from comfortable.

At around 10.00 pm, the Presiding Officer called for silence in order to read the result of the vote. We had two Parish Councillors elected: Louise Wellings and Sandra Moran.

We had gained 45 percent of the vote; our inexperience had cost us at least another five seats. The voting forms for parish and district were for eight candidates to fill the 15 seats. As we had only four candidates to vote for in each, many of the RASP supporters, thinking that the ballot paper would be void otherwise, put four Labour ticks on the same sheet, thus cancelling out their vote. Nevertheless we now had two councillors, who would have access to the Parish Council decisions and also a place at the liaison meetings held monthly at SARP UK.

On May 14, we held a protest at the gates of SARP UK to celebrate one year of struggle with this company. At 9.00 that morning about 80 of us were there with banners and placards, while the Grim Reaper walked amongst us. I had spoken with the lady at the fancy dress shop about the return of the Grim Reaper, telling her, "We are getting there, but it's taking us and the Grim Reaper a little longer than we thought."

The few tankers that there were were there now; we had stopped maybe about three or four at the most, a long way from the 30 or 40 that we could hold up before this place was almost strangled by RASP's grip over this last year. The police arrived and we slowly moved aside.

"Do you know, Mr. Moran, this is the 200th time my officers have had to come to this site in the last 12 months to you protesters," the Inspector said as he walked past me.

"Let's hope you are not saying 400th this time next year, because until we are certain that the incinerator will not operate again we will still be here," I replied.

Through June, July and August the incinerator did not restart. We had the Toxic Night Shift on a 24-hour watch, as well as the eyes of our friend Tony Milner, the night security man at Alan Cooper's coach depot. The protesters were at the gates every day, sometimes only three or four, other times a dozen or so; they would come for two or three hours then others would replace them. RASP did not trust SARP and this was why we kept watching.

There was an eerie silence on Ellisons Road through these months, like a temporary ceasefire in a war.

The beginning of September found a convoy of cars carrying around 40 RASP campaigners to County Hall in

Matlock, the home of Derbyshire County Council. We had been informed that there was to be an inauguration of some top guy and all the pomp and ceremony that went with it, and RASP intended to be there.

We arrived in the beautiful town of Matlock, one of Derbyshire's gems, but RASP were not there for the views. We climbed the steps up to the County Hall with no banners, no placards; nothing to suggest that one of the most powerful environmental groups in the UK had arrived. We looked for all the world just like another coach-load of tourists.

"We would like see the inauguration," said Margaret Ashmore to a council official inside.

"We've come a long way to see it," said May Hobson.

As I tried to keep a straight face, the official said, "Come with me. You can stand in the public gallery at the back of the auditorium, but make sure you are quiet, they don't like noise on these occasions, you know."

"Of course not, we will be quiet." Carol Dye's words were about to be proven not entirely true.

The hall where the ceremony was being held was a huge amphitheatre with all the seats going round the room in a three-quarter circle. Down the middle was an open aisle that led to the stage, where the inauguration was to be held. About 15 minutes into the ceremony, 300 or so County Councillors were giving it their rapt attention. The guy at the front, who I assumed to be the object of their attention, had the chain halfway around his neck. It was at this point that Carol Dye and myself led 40 RASP campaigners down the aisle towards the stage. Three of us managed to get on the stage – Carol, Alistair and myself – much to the horror of the security guards and more to the point the Derbyshire County Councillors watching. I was the first to speak.

"When are the Derbyshire County Council going to stop taking the money from SARP UK at Killamarsh? How long are you going to keep letting this company poison and pollute our village? How many times will you ignore us? We are, for anyone who is not aware in this hall…" I looked up towards 300 people, only my voice could be heard in the room. "We are RASP, 'Residents Against SARP Pollution' and we are here today to say that we and our children at the Sheffield Road schools are paying the real price, not SARP UK, but they are paying with their health, and the fear of another chemical disaster at the SARP UK site. It has to stop."

Carol and Alistair continued where I had finished. The security guards were just about to grab us when we leapt from the stage and retreated up the stairs, back towards the top and the exits. As we retreated, I heard Sandra and several of the RASP members call out "Judas!" Without looking I knew they had found an ex-member of our group amongst the Derbyshire councillors. The invasion was widely reported in the media the following day. The next occasion I would come to County Hall, Matlock, would be less dramatic but nevertheless very memorable.

On October 2, 1999, SARP UK announced that they had changed their name. From that day they would be known as Onyx Environmental Group.

Just over a month later, on the otherwise quiet day of November 8, the phone call came.

"Rob Waugh from *The Yorkshire Post* here, John, thought you would like to know that SARP UK, or Onyx Environmental, have issued a joint press release with the Derbyshire County Council. They are going to suspend the use of the incinerator and are in talks with the Council as to the future use of the site. They are going to announce it at a press conference this afternoon. You haven't much time – it starts in just over an hour. We have only just got this in the last few minutes, the Council and SARP obviously don't want RASP to be there."

"Thanks, Rob, I am on my way." Sandra and myself were soon heading towards Matlock. We phoned other RASP members as we drove. We arrived 15 minutes before the start time and were joined by four more RASP members: Brian and Margaret Ashmore, Wendy Wellings and her sister Eileen.

We made our way to the room where the announcement was to be made. Alan Charles, Jayne Holden and several other Killamarsh councillors who had been better informed than RASP on this occasion were present, but we had still made it and by the looks of them, much to their annoyance. The press release was handed to us as we entered. It read: "Onyx Environmental Group to Suspend Use of Killamarsh Incinerator."

The next morning, Wednesday, November 11, 1999, the front page of *The Yorkshire Post* read: "Today's announcement by the parent company of waste disposal firm SARP UK that it is to suspend use of its Killamarsh incinerator has been warmly welcomed by leading County Councillors. Onyx Environment Group spokesman David O'Connor said that they had decided to suspend the use of the incinerator and in partnership with the County Council, would examine possible alternative uses for the North East Derbyshire plant. In addition to recycling to produce secondary fuels, a favoured plan is to develop the site for the recycling of inert, nontoxic waste such as paper, cardboard, plastic and construction materials. Onyx has promised to work with the County Council towards the possible establishment of a furniture recycling project. This would provide both new jobs for local unemployed people and good quality second-hand furniture and household appliances to needy families in the coalfield area.

"Council leader Martin Doughty said, 'Onyx's decision to suspend use of the incinerator shows an innovative approach to dealing with problems following on from the two chemical leaks in May last year.' Killamarsh County Councillor Alan Charles said, 'Onyx should be congratulated for seeking an innovative solution.'"

Both men were singing from the same song sheet, the wording of their speeches almost identical. We concluded that was what "toeing the party line" was all about.

Sandra and myself drove home the 30 miles or so to Killamarsh that night and we were both in a strange mood. We were both still angry, not great company. Looking back, we were like two punch-drunk boxers – we had fought this company for the best part of two years, day after day, and now that they had told us it was over, the anger would not go away. It was as if we refused to leave the ring. What should have been a great celebration at that moment in time didn't seem like one.

Chapter Twenty-One

People Power

The Yorkshire Post said that the decision by SARP UK to shut down its hazardous waste incinerator marked a famous victory for people power. In the November 11, 1999 edition, there was a full-page photograph and the following article, in which Rob Waugh looked back on "a remarkable grassroots campaign by the residents in the former mining village of Killamarsh in North East Derbyshire".

"On the face of it, it wasn't much of a contest. On one side, a huge multinational company with headquarters in Paris, on the other the ordinary residents of a former mining village near Sheffield. But this week's announcement by chemical waste company SARP UK that it is shutting down its hazardous waste incinerator marks a famous victory for the people of Killamarsh. They totally refused to accept the odds. Over the last 18 months they rarely gave the company a moment's peace. Out of the seven processes the plant operated at the time of the two infamous toxic chemical leaks in May last year only one remains. Most importantly of all, the incinerator, complete with its 50-metre chimney, which dominates the skyline, is now to go. For John Moran, the Killamarsh milkman for many years and one of the mainstays of 'Residents Against SARP Pollution', the almost complete capitulation by the company has opened his eyes to what ordinary people can achieve with enough determination and organisation. Over the last 18 months the protesters have never let up. They have marched through the village, fielded candidates in local elections, travelled to the headquarters of parent company Vivendi in Paris, took it to the Houses of Parliament and the EU in Brussels, trespassed on the site to highlight holes in security fences and breaches of emission levels by the incinerator, bombarded the Environment Agency with complaints at every opportunity and kept a picket by the site gates just about every night since May last year. It's no exaggeration to say that the orange cloud of noxious gas which belched out of the site and drifted towards south-east Sheffield last year not only horrified local people but went on to change some of their lives.

"'It centralised everybody's thought. I knew I hated the place, I knew lots of people complained about it, but I could never have believed the way people would respond,' said Mr.

Moran. 'It's partly because it's a close-knit village where most people know everybody else, it's an old mining village and also people knew the campaign was well organised from the beginning.'

"Mr. Moran's own life changed without doubt, particularly at the height of the campaign. Already up at 3.30 am to do the milk round, he would be back soon after 8.00 am and spend hours on the phone campaigning. Sleep was gradually getting squeezed to two or three hours a night. 'The company thought we would go away after six or eight weeks, the very fact we were still campaigning as hard 18 months later must have come as a shock to them.'

"Despite the seriousness of the issue, the 18-month haul has not been without humour – with particular highlights being the time a SARP tanker left the site with a chemist still on top checking the labelling and the incongruous sight of a young lad in a Sheffield Wednesday shirt who found himself sitting in the President's chair when campaigners forced a showdown into Vivendi's boardroom in Paris. But most of all, said Mr. Moran, the campaign has taught those involved what ordinary people can achieve. 'We learned how you can take ordinary people – a milkman, painter and decorator, railway workers, retired people, people with no technical knowledge – and give them a year to 18 months' involvement in a campaign and they can not only hold their own with the experts but frighten them. It raised people above the level they had been all their lives. I wondered why I had been dropping milk bottles for 28 years, yet I could now converse with directors of a huge multinational company, they were just ordinary people, that was the lesson. We learned that if ordinary people stick together and are determined enough they can move anything.'"

Chapter Twenty-Two

The Days of Reckoning

Just before Christmas of 1999, *The Sheffield Star* reported on another important milestone in the battle. The headline was: "SARP UK Fined £270,000 for Waste Leaks." The article went on to say, "Residents Against SARP Pollution (RASP) at Killamarsh were celebrating today after SARP UK was landed with a £270,000 bill for two pollution scares. SARP UK has been fined £120,000 with costs of £150,000 after admitting four charges relating to two incidents last May when fumes were released over Killamarsh.

"Residents Against SARP Pollution spokesman John Moran praised the severity of the sentence. 'We are pleased the courts have dealt severely with them and hope it may deter other companies from taking chances with communities and other people's lives,' he said after the case.

"A joint prosecution was brought by the Environment Agency and the Health and Safety Executive. Judge John Wait criticised SARP UK for their 'ignorance' during the removal and storage of concentrated acid mixtures at the Killamarsh plant. The first incident started on May 14 after SARP took their first delivery of acid from British Aerospace, Derby Crown Court heard. A tanker carrying the mix of nitric acid and sulphuric acid had inadequate seals, which began to melt after the vehicle was left overnight at the Killamarsh site. Prosecutor Mark Harris said staff decided to transfer the mixture into a tank as quickly as possible, but this exacerbated the problem. He said, 'The pipe used to convey the liquid also melted and the mixtures began to escape in large quantities, causing a fire and then a noxious 300-foot cloud which rose above Killamarsh. The emergency services were called and the public were told to stay indoors and keep their windows and doors closed. It took firefighters two and a half hours to deal with the situation.

"'The second leak on May 30 occurred when a tank containing a mixture of hydrochloric acid, hydrofluoric acid and sulphuric acid was added to other acids. The acids reacted with each other and there could have well been a crack in the tank, which the mixture quickly exploited.'

"The court was shown a video of the large cloud of orange noxious smoke drifting towards the surrounding area and the Rother Valley Country Park. The incidents sparked a community protest campaign by Residents Against SARP Pollution, known as RASP, which has forced the closure of almost all of the plant and the incinerator. Rhodri Price Lewis for SARP UK said the company 'sincerely apologised' to the residents for the problems they had caused."

Two weeks later on January 15, 2000, Leigh Environmental, SARP UK's predecessor on the Killamarsh site, were in court once again. The headline in *The Sheffield Star* read, "Poison Waste Report 'Faked' – False Records Cost Company £100,000." The article said: "Waste company Leigh Environmental has been landed with a £100,000 fine for faking records of dangerous wastes at its Sheffield offices. The punishment was imposed by magistrates in Telford after they admitted seven breaches of landfill conditions on two tips in the Midlands. The breaches came after the Environment Agency was sent records of dangerous waste levels which had been falsified by a worker at Leigh's offices in Beighton near Sheffield. Agency workers launched a two-and-a-half-year investigation after a tipoff by an employee at the Coalmoor landfill site near Telford. Magistrates heard figures for oil, cyanide and cadmium were most frequently changed. Records of arsenic, lead phenol and nickel were altered. Samples taken at two sites were analysed by an independent laboratory and used by Leigh to calculate the ratio of household to 'difficult' waste including hazardous substances. Results should have been supplied to the Agency.

But the court heard the sample results had been falsified at the Beighton offce. In all, 252 out of 517 reports of levels of 'difficult' wastes passed to the Agency were false.

"After the hearing, Environment Agency official Steve Morley said, 'The case was extremely serious. If the amounts of "difficult" wastes had continued to be dumped and figures falsified there was a risk of serious environmental damage occurring, if it had not already done so.' They were fined £87,500 and ordered to pay £20,552 costs.

"*The Yorkshire Post* and *The Sheffield Star* both asked RASP Parish Councillor Sandra Moran for comment about this latest court appearance of Leigh Environmental. Her response was, 'We at RASP made identical allegations last year about falsification of data and illegal waste loads being dumped here at the SARP UK plant. The Environment Agency in the West Midlands appear to have investigated such claims more vigorously than their colleagues from Rotherham Environment Agency did here in Killamarsh. Last year we know that 20 tonnes of arsenic went somewhere on this site, never mind all the talk of "clerical error", this prosecution verifies that statement. Though we at RASP forced the closure of the landfill site last year, we fear that the waste tipped there will create serious problems in the future to the water table in and around Killamarsh.'"

It was June 2, 2000, just over two years since the two orange clouds. I had a visit from a BBC Radio Sheffield reporter. She sat in my front garden and the interview went something like this.

"Well, Mr. Moran, we are sitting here today on a beautiful day, not a cloud in the sky, especially orange ones. What can you tell us about life here after the campaign that your environmental group Residents Against SARP Pollution fought against the toxic waste company SARP UK?"

"We at RASP and the residents of the village all know that we are feeling healthier thanks to the closure of six out of the seven sites at SARP UK. RASP has done a survey in the village that shows the number of people with breathing problems has fallen sharply since the closure of the toxic waste incinerator. Local GPs and North East Derbyshire Health Authority are also being challenged to make public statistics on asthma levels and inhaler prescriptions. We believe that use of inhalers and asthma levels are falling. I have four lads who work for me on my milk round and three years ago they all had to use inhalers, I have not seen one of them have to use an inhaler in the last six months. We believe the closure of the incinerator is having a major positive effect on the health of the village. It closed down on November 8, but it hasn't burnt toxics since the incidents in May 1998."

The reporter then said, "The Derbyshire Health Authority have announced that they are going to issue results for a survey of schools in the area regarding asthma and inhalers, what is your comment?"

"We will not hold our breath here at RASP, we remember the words of our friend from the Welsh Valleys, Dr. Dick van Steenis, when it comes to trusting Health Authorities."

Almost two weeks later, on June 13, 2000, SARP UK, now known as Onyx Environmental Group, announced that they had made the decision to give up the right to operate the incinerator at the Killamarsh plant. Responding to this a press conference, I said, "We welcome this announcement; it has taken our campaign group just over two years to force this company to do this, we now await the final removal of the incinerator chimney and then the job will be done."

The humiliation for SARP UK was almost complete, but they were to hold out for almost another two years on that front. On March 21, 2002, just under four years since the start of our campaign, the toxic waste incinerator that stood at the site was pulled down.

Chapter Twenty-Three

Life After RASP

The final meeting of Residents Against SARP Pollution was held in the Crown on July 20, 2002. Wendy Wellings opened the meeting.

"Tonight there is only one item on the agenda – to decide what we are to do with the funds of the group. Currently they stand at £1150.51."

The group decided that we would donate all of it to the Sheffield Children's Hospital cancer fund. That night we finally celebrated together; we had become the only environmental group in the UK to close down and remove a toxic waste incinerator by the power of protest.

Looking around the room that night, there was a touch of sadness, knowing that the group might never be together again. The last four years in RASP had been a roller-coaster of a ride. When Alistair in 1998 said, "You will go where you have never been before, you will do things you never thought you would do, you will say things you never thought you would say," they were the truest words spoken in our campaign.

I would miss my role as Press Officer, something that I ended up finding very easy – it felt as if I had done it all my life. I would miss the camaraderie of all my fellow campaigners that fighting together for a common cause brings. That's what I would miss, and I think that all the group felt the same.

The next morning I made my way to the fancy dress shop on Sheffield Road, to take the Grim Reaper home. He had been with us just over four years.

In the years that have passed we all went our separate ways. Alistair Tice of the Socialist Party is still leading campaigns all over this area for working-class people with very little Trade Union representation. Rebecca Fryer has been a bus driver for First Line for the last 18 years and is still very active in the Socialist Party. Ann Nettleship still lives in the village and has three grandchildren. When I spoke with her recently she told me, "Life is good." Carol Dye remarried and is now Carol Lacey; she is a Killamarsh Parish Councillor and is putting up this year for the District Council.

Her husband Tony Lacey is also a parish councillor. Allison Sampson sadly passed away in 2017 and her husband Kevin moved away from Killamarsh. When I spoke with him recently I found out he is now a very proud grandfather. Tony Ward and his wife Ann are still very involved in the community, Tony also helps with the Killamarsh Heritage Society. Their daughter Helen Robinson helped me greatly to trace RASP members. The baby in the pram on the children's march holding the banner, Helen's son Thomas Robinson, is now 25 years old and a door and window fitter for a company in Sheffield. He is also a qualified football coach to the Killamarsh Dynamos children's teams, looking out for another like Millie Bright of Chelsea and England, one of ours from Killamarsh. Big thanks to Wez Mathers, my old milk lad, for help in contacting members of RASP. Terry Hobson has passed away, but his wife May is going strong at 86. The man with the black beret, one of our leading campaigners Brian Ashmore has also passed away, and his wife Margaret lives in a care home at nearby Eckington. Brenda Glossop and Myra Turner still live on Primrose Close and remain great friends. Brenda Hancock, wearing a mask in one of the campaign photos a long time before COVID made them fashionable, is still living in the village, as is her close friend and RASP member Liz, who ran a hairdressing salon on Kirkcroft Lane, and her son Ben. Steve Martin and his wife Sue also still live in the village. Roger Barraclough and his wife Linda had until recently still been running the Crown pub, they have now retired. Sadly Killamarsh lost its poet 'Owd Tup', aka Dave Froggatt, when he passed away in 2017. Alan Charles still lives in Killamarsh after serving as Chairman of the Education Committee from 1999, he then went on to be the Police and Crime Commissioner for Derbyshire in 2009 till he retired in 2016. Alan Charles was the only elected member of the Derbyshire County Council who ever stood with RASP. David Milson is now retired from his job at Sheffield Town Hall. Dr. Jon Dale is very active as Branch Secretary East Midlands for the Unite union in the NHS. Ann and Trevor Cockerill went to live in Worksop; we are still in touch. Ken Coates MEP sadly passed away in 2010 aged 79. My daughter Faye left Killamarsh after the campaign ended and went to work in the wine industry in Bristol, where she still lives with her partner, Stephen.

Among the journalists who supported the campaign through their written words, Graham Readfearn of *The Yorkshire Post* now a leading environmental writer for *The Guardian* based in Brisbane, Australia. His colleague on *The Yorkshire Post* Rob Waugh is still an active, award-winning journalist, while Steve Caddy of *The Sheffield Star* left the paper in 2001 and went on to become editor of *Pure Peak* magazine at Matlock. I want to thank Nicola Smith of *The Derbyshire Times*, Mike Ellis of our local paper *The Eckington Leader*, who was the main reporter with us in Paris and sadly passed away not long after our campaign ended, and also *The Socialist* newspaper, a big supporter of our campaign. While we are with the press, a big thank you to Claire Lewis, the current editor of *The Sheffield Star* and her colleague Jane Salt, who kindly supplied me with photos from their archives that appear in this book. Also I would like to thank my editor Melanie Scott for her enthusiasm, attention to detail and patience in the preparation of this book for publishing.

And my special thanks to the unknown person who carried that Sainsbury's carrier bag to my gate in the early hours of that July morning in 1998.

It is only fair at this point to say what happened to Vivendi. They changed their name once again to Veolia in 2003. The intervening years have been controversial: water privatisations of different communities from Seattle to Alabama to Buenos Aires, Europe to Asia have not gone well. There has been trouble in Israel regarding the building of a tramway from East Jerusalem to the West Bank and their involvement against the human rights of the Palestinians living in the occupied territories. BDS (Boycott, Divestment and Sanctions) activists around the world forced Veolia to divest from the Israeli market after causing it to lose $20 billion worth of contracts for its complicity in Israel's human rights violations.

On June 25, 2012, a New York jury slapped a $954.6 million fine on Vivendi for fraud. On August 7, 2014, Veolia had 150 tonnes of a chemical weapons stockpile from Syria, a stockpile that President Assad had threatened to use on his own people, delivered to Ellesmere Port, Merseyside for its destruction at its Bridges Road incinerator. One may ask why a country as small and densely populated as the UK is still importing such dangerous toxic waste chemicals from all over the world.

Lastly, what happened to the man who once sent me a letter, Jean-Marie Messier, CEO of Vivendi? In 2002 the BBC World Service described him as 'the man with the ambition to take over the world'; within five years he had taken Vivendi from a sleepy water company and turned it into the second biggest media conglomerate on earth, Vivendi-Universal. Unfortunately, like a few men in history before him he came back to earth when he recorded a €15 billion loss in 2002 and was dismissed. I will always keep his letter, it's not every day you will get a letter from a "man who had the ambition to take over the world" and almost did.

And myself? In the years after RASP, in 2005, I became seriously ill and only just survived, and this was what prompted me to sell the milk round and to retire, much to the relief of Sandra. We finished up in southern Spain, in a beautiful old Spanish town called Guardamar del Segura on the Mediterranean. We have lived here for the last 16 years.

The reason I wrote this book was that I wanted everyone that was involved in RASP to be remembered, as a community that stood together, a "blueprint" for all future community protests. We had asked the Killamarsh Parish Council in 2002 if we could hang a plaque in the Village Centre to remember the achievements of RASP. They refused.

This book is dedicated to all members of that environmental group known as RASP (Residents Against SARP Pollution) at Killamarsh.

Printed in Great Britain
by Amazon